SCULPTURE IN MY HEAD

SCULPTURE IN MY HEAD

A collection of lyrics, poems and thoughts that breathe in me.

By JOHN D. FITZPATRICK

Writers Club Press

San Jose   New York   Lincoln   Shanghai

SCULPTURE IN MY HEAD

A collection of lyrics, poems and thoughts that breathe in me.

Writers Club Press
an imprint of iUniverse, Inc.

For information address:
iUniverse, Inc.
5220 S. 16th St., Suite 200
Lincoln, NE 68512
www.iuniverse.com

ISBN: 0-595-20961-0

Printed in the United States of America

DEDICATION

This body of work is dedicated to: Shelley, Jim, Lana, Scott, Mark, Mildred, Frank, Max, Lenida, Brigette, Madeline, Jenny, My Extended Family, Matt, Dave, Johanna, Terry, All Of My Other Friends, Bono, Good Times, Good Cigars, Love and Guinness (the dog and the beer)

CONTENTS

PREFACE

The enclosed sampling of work is an ongoing series of seemingly, never-ending projects in my head. It is a pilgrimage (if you will) of thought, but it is also a display case of my talent as a writer, of which is a serious attempt to emotionally move others.

My lofty goals are to one day be paid for my work and to actually have a musical artist or group use my lyrics or poems in a song or songs. I believe that "good" lyrics and "good" phrases are hard to manufacture, but if obtained, will certainly last in the listener's/reader's mind for great lengths of time. Until then, I will continue to write, growing in knowledge, refining in form and hopefully capturing new events and experiences in a unique way.

If you wish to contact me with comment and/or to use any of the enclosed works in this book, please do so by writing to me at my email address: irishcorona@onebox.com.

Thank you for any interest that you have, had or may have in my work.

ACKNOWLEDGEMENTS

A special thank you to my parents, who always told me that I could achieve anything in life, and who also shelled-out a lot of time and a lot of bucks to give me the tools necessary to survive in this world. To those people, over the years, who have supported me and my many choices, good or bad. A big shout-out to my editor and "SM" Shelley Thompson. Also, thank you to the people, places and events that have inspired me and seemingly motivated me to write the works in this book. Lastly, to those little voices in my head, the ones that God placed there, of which I started tuning into at age thirteen.

LYRICS

(POSITIVE)

CUT ABOVE

BLUE-JEAN GIRL WITH A FADED SMILE
WALK INTO MY LIFE, I'LL WALK YOU DOWN THE AISLE

YOU SEE THERE'S NO GOLD AROUND MY FINGER
I'M STILL WAITING FOR GOD TO BRING HER

I NEED TO BE SAVED FROM THE PAIN THAT BREAKS ME
TRAP ME, THEN WRAP ME IN YOUR WHITE-LIGHT ENERGY

YOU'RE A CUT ABOVE
THE ONE THAT I LOVE
A HIT TELEVISION SHOW IN MY HEAD
I'M A SPIDER IN YOUR WEB
YOU'RE A CUT ABOVE
A CUT ABOVE

SAW YOU FROM GROUND LEVEL, THOUGHT YOU WERE AN ANGEL
DON'T TREAT ME LIKE THE DEVIL, I'VE ALREADY BEEN TO HELL

LIKE WIND TO SAND YOU SHIFT ME
YOUR BEAUTY BUILDS WALLS THEN IMPRISONS ME

LET ME BE THE ONE TO TUCK YOU IN…SHOW YOU TRUTH
THEN DIRTY YOUR DISHWATER WITH MY FORK AND SPOON

YOU'RE A CUT ABOVE
THE ONE THAT I LOVE
A SONG IN A BOOK OF HYMNS
LIGHT THAT NEVER DIMS
YOU'RE A CUT ABOVE
A CUT ABOVE

BE THE FLAME TO MY CANDLE, LIGHT MY WAY
PAINT MY HEART LIKE A VANDAL…COVER THE GRAY

COME SEE THE ROOM MY HEART HAS BUILT FOR YOU
COME TO MY DOORWAY…WALK THROUGH

YOU'RE A CUT ABOVE
THE ONE THAT I LOVE
A POLISHED STONE…
PUNCTUATION UNKNOWN
YOU'RE A CUT ABOVE
A CUT ABOVE

WHEN DOES LOVE BEGIN

TONIGHT SHE IS LIKE A MARIGOLD
TO FRAGILE TO HOLD

SHE PUTS ON HER BEST PERFUME
THE KIND THAT FILLS THE ROOM

TANGLES HER SMILE IN YOUR EYES
WAVES HER HAND PAST HER HAIR TWICE

YOU IMAGINE…
THE FEEL OF HER SKIN
WILL YOU TAKE HER FIRST COMMUNION
WHEN DOES LOVE BEGIN

SHE STIRS THE ICE IN YOUR GLASS
YOU SEEM TO MELT WITH EVERY PASS

HEAVEN'S WHITE ROSE
THE ONE GOD CHOSE

HER BEAUTY GRAVITY
HER DISEASE INCURABILITY

SHE'S TEMPTATION
FRUSTRATION…

COOL WATERS FLOW OVER ME
HER SHORES OFFER SAFETY
WILL I SWIM IN
WHEN DOES LOVE BEGIN

NEVER CERTAIN OF MY EVALUATION
IS SHE MY SALVATION

OFF-BALANCE WHEN SHE IS NEAR
IT COULD BE CAUTION, IT COULD BE FEAR

I LOVE THE WAY SHE SAVES ME
NO MORE DRUDGERY

SHE DEFINES COMMON MOMENTS
SHE HAS BECOME MY SIXTH SENSE
NO MEDIUM CAN CAPTURE HER VISION
WHEN DOES LOVE BEGIN

BUTTERFLY

SHE'S LIKE A BULLET WOUND IN MY SIDE…
WHEN SHE CAN'T DECIDE

SHE'S A SHARK THAT CIRCLES ME
A LAUGH THAT COMES EVENTUALLY

WILL WE EVER SEE EYE TO EYE
WILL SHE BECOME MY BUTTERFLY

WATER ONLY CLEANSES THE SKIN
DIRTY THOUGHTS STILL GET IN
PULLED THROUGH THEN PUSHED OUT
TOSSED AROUND BY FEAR AND DOUBT

SHE'S THE STATIC IN MY BRAIN
MY BLOOD VEIN

SHE'S A SEQUEL TO MY PAST
MONEY THAT DOESN'T LAST

SHE LIKES TO FLY FROM HER COCOON
SOMETIMES CIRCLE AROUND THE ROOM

SHE MAKES SURE OTHERS SEE HER FLIGHT
WEARS NOTHING BUT BRIGHT COLORS AGAINST HER CANVAS AT NIGHT
ALTHOUGH SHE HAS BOUTS WITH DIFFERENT SORTS
SHE NEVER LOSES SIGHT OF LOVE'S COHORTS

SHE'S THE SWIRLING SNOW
THE POTTED PLANT THAT NEEDS TO GROW

OH TOMORROW…THAT'S WHAT SHE OFTEN SAID
AS TIME HITS HER IN THE GUT AND KICKS ME IN THE HEAD

SILENCE THROUGH THE NIGHT, CAN'T EVER MAKE IT RIGHT
THOUGHTS NEED TO BREATHE…LET YOUR APPETITE EAT

I'M THE INSECT IN HER PINCERS
A DINNER OF SEVENTY-TWO INCHES
BUT A DESSERT PLATE I'LL NEVER BE
WHEN CONFIDENCE MELTS SO RAPIDLY

SHE'S A CABLE CHANNEL I BARELY RECEIVE
A LIE WHICH IS SOMETIMES HARD TO BELIEVE

SHE WRAPPED ME IN HER WEB…LEFT TO DANGLE
SPUN FROM CONVERSATION HER WORDS ENTANGLE

SENDING MY SOUL INTO THE SUN, SHE'S THE ONE
MY BUTTERFLY…MY EQUILIBRIUM

OUR LOVE

SPECIAL DATES, SPECIAL TIMES…MANY MEMORIES PAST
SO MANY HILLS, SO MANY CLIMBS, WAS IT REALLY MEANT TO LAST

EVENTS ONCE COOKED IN THE OVEN NOW COOL ON THE TABLE
YOUR HAND STILL FEELS THE BURN, BUT THE ANGER IS STABLE

OUR LOVE, A LADDER-STEP HIGHER…
A REACH WHICH CAN HOLD OR LET GO OF THE FIRE
OUR LOVE…LET US BREATHE WITHOUT AIR
ANTY-UP, LOW STAKES WITH GREAT YIELD IS RARE

WHAT ONCE FED THE PAIN INSIDE NOW PURGES LOST HOPE…
YOUR INTELLECT, ONCE A TRAIN-WRECK, HAS ABANDONED THE HANGMAN'S ROPE

A NEW LIGHT HAS SHOWN BEYOND THE DARKEST LINE
YOU RETURNED TO ME WHAT I TOOK AWAY…WITHOUT FINE

OUR LOVE, THE TIME IS RIGHT FOR A PASSION STREAK
IT'S NO LONGER A FRIDAY-TO-SUNDAY STORY-WEEK
OUR LOVE REVELS UNDER THE LIGHT OF A NEW DAY
HEAVY PASSION SINKS INTO NEW GROUND, A LOVE-BAY

LIFE IS SOMETIMES COBBLESTONE…. WE CLEAR THE HOLES IN THE STREET
SHADOWS WHERE LIGHT ONCE SHOWN USE TO FILL SPACES SO NEAT

DESIRE ONCE DRIED-UP NOW WAKES WITH THE RAIN
REVIVED, AGAIN RAISED, WE NO LONGER SLEEP NEXT TO THE DRAIN

OUR LOVE, A BACKWARDS PLOT TO FIND WHAT'S LOST
BURIED AT THE BOTTOM OF DOUBT WE PAID THAT COST
OUR LOVE, DON'T QUESTION THE TEST, QUESTION THE PLAN
OUR LOVE, TWO PINCHES OF SUGAR AND TWO PINCHES OF SAND

SIGNALS

SHOULD I…
GIVE HER A TRY…

WORDS CAN'T CELEBRATE WHAT SHE BRINGS TO THIS PLACE
SUBTLETY, WRAPPED IN FIRE, SHE SHOWS NO WORRY IN HER FACE

WHAT IS ONE TO DO WHEN FEELINGS SWALLOW YOUR HEAD
WHEN THE COGS TURN, YOUR BLOOD BURNS…AND FEAR SLEEPS IN YOUR BED

SIGNALS…AN ARRAY OF LAUGHTER AND LIGHT
SIGNALS…WILL YOU LEARN ANYTHING TONIGHT
DID YOU EVER THINK IT WOULD COME TO THIS
A SMILE, A TOUCH, THE NEED TO KISS

I WANT TO WIN HER ELECTION
BECOME THE BREASTPLATE OF HER PROTECTION

TO STORM RIVAL TOWERS IN HER NAME
TO CHANGE AND TO NEVER BE THE SAME

STILL WATERS RIPPLE AROUND HER
SHE'S ALL I SEE…EVERYTHING BUT US IS A BLUR

SIGNALS…CAN I HAVE THE CHANCE…
SIGNALS…WILL I KNOW WHEN TO DANCE
I HAVE JUST ENOUGH ENERGY TO SEE THIS THROUGH
IF IT'S RIGHT WITH ME…IS IT RIGHT FOR YOU

A WINE NOT OFTEN TASTED BY THESE LIPS
HER VOICE A BOUQUET OF SHALLOW SIPS

STEADY MAN…OR YOU'LL GO OFF COURSE
SHOW INTEREST BUT AVOID THAT POWERFUL FORCE

SHOW HER THAT CIRCUMSTANCE WAS NOT LEFT TO FATE
DISPLAY NO WORRIES AND SHE'LL NOT HESITATE

SIGNALS…HER TIRES COULD RUN-OVER MY NECK
SIGNALS…BUT I NEED HER MUSIC IN MY TAPE DECK
IT SIMPLY COMES DOWN TO PEOPLE WHO SEE OR DON'T
OPPORTUNITY MIXES LOVE TOGETHER, FEAR AND INSECURITY WON'T

THESE WORDS

EVERY NOW AND THEN TIME CAN STOP A HEARTBEAT
WHEN YOUR SENSES SWELL AND THE MIND AND BODY MEET

FOR ONCE YOU SEE WHAT GOD MEANT YOU TO SEE
BEAUTY AND GRACE HAVE COME TOGETHER SPIRITUALLY

THESE WORDS CAN'T TELL OF MY LOVE
THESE WORDS WON'T EXPLAIN WHAT I'M THINKING OF
SUMMER IS THE SEASON THAT YOU BRING TO ME
WINTER IS THE REASON I NEED YOUR SYMPATHY

FEELING INVINCIBLE, I APPROACHED HER AND SPOKE HER NAME
RADIANT, SHE FLICKERED WHEN I TRIED TO TOUCH HER FLAME

LATER, I FOLLOWED HER TRAIN DOWN THE TRACKS
MAYBE I WENT TOO FAR, ACCEPTING FICTION FOR FACTS

THESE WORDS CAN'T TELL OF MY LOVE
THESE WORDS WON'T EXPLAIN WHAT I'M THINKING OF
SHADOWED HANDS RAISED TOWARDS THE LIGHT…
AS A WEIGHTED SPIRIT TRIES TO REACH ITS ORIGINAL HEIGHT

SOMETIMES SHE'S SUCH THE GIRL BEHIND THE GLASS
SOMEONE I CAN SEE CLEARLY, BUT PROTECTED AS I PASS

OH…I BELIEVE THAT LOVE CAN FILL ANY DEEP WOUND
JUST PLANT THE SEED, NEVER HEED AND ALWAYS STAY-TUNED

THESE WORDS CAN'T TELL OF MY LOVE
THESE WORDS WON'T EXPLAIN WHAT I'M THINKING OF
AWAKENED FROM THE PAST WITH A BOLD SHOVE
THESE WORDS CAN'T TELL OF MY LOVE

HEAL

LIKE THE ELDEST TREE, YOUR LINES RUN DEFINED AND DEEP
YOUR LIMBS ACHING FROM FORGOTTEN FRUIT AND THE PRESENCE YOU KEEP

CALENDAR DAYS START AND FINISH WITH A PATTERN MISMATCH…
AND THE LIFE YOU ONCE FLAVORED NOW SEEMS TO SOUR THE BATCH

TRY TO HEAL, DON'T QUESTION THE REASON…
YOUR SKIN IS YOUR SIN, ANGER THE SEASON
PUNCH A HOLE THROUGH THE BAG TONIGHT
OUTSIDE YOUR PUPPET-SKIN YOU'LL SEE NEW LIGHT

THE STATIC ROLLS ON A WHEEL IN YOUR HEAD…REVERSE IT
CHANGE YOUR DESTRUCTION AND GET OUT OF BED…. CURSE A BIT

SHOE-BOX-LOVE WAS THE STINT THAT WORE-OUT YOUR SOUL
TIME TO TIE NEW LACES AROUND YOUR SEPARATED WHOLE

TRY TO HEAL, STITCH THE CUTS CLOSED
EMBRACE THE NEW AND LISTEN TO THE NOW PROPOSED
JUST ANOTHER TOASTED MOMENT…GLASSES RAISED TO THE SKY
WHEN LOVE-FILLED WE DRINK TO FOREVER, WITHOUT…WE DRINK TO DIE

PUT THIS MOOD ON YOUR EXPENSE ACCOUNT,…LABEL IT DOUBT
PRESS YOURSELF FROM THE FLOOR, NOW DETOUR FROM THIS ROUTE

YOU WONDER IN AMAZEMENT AT THE FALL OF YOUR ROME
YOUR RULE NO LONGER BUILDS CASTLES OR POLISHES THE CHROME

TRY TO HEAL, UNWRAP SPACE AND PATIENCE
GIFTS THAT YOU'VE SEALED ONCE AGAIN MAKE SENSE
WHETHER IT WAS ACTION OR REST WHICH CREATED THIS SPACE
WIPE YOUR FEET AT THE DOOR AND RE-ENTER GOD'S GRACE

ILLOGICAL

SHE'S COCA-COLA AND I'M 7-UP…
I HAVE A BOWL OF LOVE, SHE HAS A CUP

SOMETIMES OUR PASSION IS RECREATION
OTHER TIMES IT'S JUST RANDOM EXPLOITATION

SHE'S ILLOGICAL
SHE BREAKS MY WILL
SHE BUILDS PRISONS AROUND ME
SHE'S A SHARK'S FIN IN THE OPEN SEA

SHE EATS ME LIKE A SIT-DOWN-DINNER…
WITH HER NAPKIN IN HAND I SURRENDER AS A BEGINNER

WHO KNEW THAT SHE WOULD COME ALONG…WILD FIRE
STAINLESS, FORGED BY HEAT, BUT WITH A COOL DESIRE

SHE'S ILLOGICAL
SHE LOVES ME TO DEATH UNTIL
SHE'S THE WARMTH I KNOW, THE LAND I CALL HOME
SHE'S PORTIA TO CAESAR, SHE'S RULING ROME

HER APPEARANCE IS NINE TENTHS OF THE LAW
PUT YOUR HAND IN THE HORNET'S NEST, IT COMES OUT RAW

A CHANGE IN COMFORT IS A GOOD THING
TO JUGGLE EMOTIONS CAN BE A SEASONAL WINTER TO SPRING

SHE'S ILLOGICAL
DON'T CHANGES EVERYTHING THAT YOU WILL
THE NIGHT IS CALLING…TOUCH ME BLACK
SHE'S ILLOGICAL, SEE HER SMILE WHEN ON THE ATTACK

BRIDGES

SEE THE CITY LIGHTS AS THEY BEGIN TO WAKE…
FROM ATOP THIS POINT MY APPETITE MEETS INTAKE

CONNECTING WITH YOU IN A DIFFERENT WAY…
WE COME TOGETHER ACROSS A WIDENED BAY

BRIDGES, CONNECTING LAND AND LIVES
MAKING SPACE DISAPPEAR THROUGH STRENGTH AND SIZE
BRIDGES OF CONCRETE, STEEL…EVEN SKIN
THEY TRANSPORT DREAMS TO VACANCIES, DISGRACE FROM SIN

SOMETIMES THERE ARE HOLES IN THE SKYWAY
PROBLEMS THAT COULD LEAD TO DECAY

WHAT YOUR SENSES OFTEN REVEAL AS SAFE, THE DARK MAY HIDE
A SAFE PASSAGE FOR YOU WILL DEPEND UPON WHAT'S INSIDE

BRIDGES, A METHOD TO YOUR MEANS
THE GROUND BELOW IS HIGHER THAN IT SEEMS
BRIDGES…WITH ICE OR DESERT DRY…
THE WAY THAT YOU CROSS REQUIRES A WATCHFUL EYE

WITH THIS BRIDGE, I GIVE YOU MY HEART…WHOLE
APART FROM MY BODY, NEAR THE CENTER OF MY SOUL

PLACE YOUR HANDS TO MY MOUTH,…NO SPEECHES
BE THANKFUL FOR THIS LINK AND THE GAP IT BREACHES

BRIDGES, THEIR HELP MAY LEAD YOU TO FIND…
PASSAGE OVER PROBLEMS,…CANYONS IN YOUR MIND
BRIDGES, BUILT BY HOPE OR DESTROYED BY DESIRE
OPENESS CREATES STRENGTH, DECEIT…A WICKED FIRE

TENDER HEART (1)

TENDER HEART YOU SURROUND ME WITH A HIGHER LOVE
HEADLIGHTS, BRIGHT NIGHTS,…I'M ON AN EAGLE'S FLIGHT ABOVE

STATUE OF BEAUTY, YOUR TORCH STAYS RAISED THROUGH THE RAIN
A LITTLE CUTIE, A CHEERLEADER…A CAPITAL GAIN

TENDER HEART,…WILLING TO GIVE AT ANYTIME
A TEN ON A TEN-SCALE, A DOLLAR TO MY DIME
SOMETHING ON DISPLAY, YET A PRIVATE ART
NEVER AFRAID, MY DEFENDER…TENDER HEART

THOSE EYES…RADAR, I BLIP ON YOUR SCREEN
NAKED SKIES, MY OWN SPACE TO CLOUD-LAY…UNSEEN

ALWAYS WALKING WITH ME, OUR SPEED CONSTANT AND ALIKE
YOUR OUTLINE, SPIRITUAL AND SENSUAL…FEELINGS SO TIGHT

TENDER HEART, SHE CAN SHOW SLIDES TO THE BLIND
A WOMAN,…A HUMAN WITH A DEEPENED MIND
IT'S THE KIND OF THING ONLY GOD CAN START
MY GLASS OF EVERYTHING POURED BY THAT TENDER HEART

SHE'S OPEN TO ME…BOTH SPIRIT AND PURSE
SHE CURES MY SICKNESS AND KILLS THE WORSE

ALWAYS MAKES A PATH TO THE GOOD AND THE JUST
INSIDE, SHE TILLS MY WILL AND SCATTERS THE DUST

TENDER HEART, A COUNTRY WITH HIGH-RENT LAND
SHE GIVES ME SHELTER, SHELTER IN THE PALM OF HER HAND
MY LIFE, A LOST LETTER FOUND IN HER MAIL CART
SHE PAYS MY POSTAGE,…THEN POSTS ME TO HER HEART

THAT

SHE'S A PASSENGER OUT OF VIEW
YET SHE'S STARING RIGHT AT YOU

TEMPTED BY THE TINTED GLASS
SHE ASKS THE DRIVER IF HE WILL PASS

SIDE-BY-SIDE THE CARS ALMOST KISS
THE ROAD NO LONGER HUMS BUT SINGS OF HAPPINESS

WHAT'S THAT FEELING
HAS YOUR HEART HIT THE LOW-BEAM CEILING
PASSION'S VIEW IS A TUNNELED-VIEW
...ALWAYS TRYING TO GUESS WHEN THE SURFACE WILL SHINE THROUGH

A BLACK LIMO TO YOUR LEFT NOW SHADOWS THE SUN
YOU THINK THAT YOU HAVE SEEN A VISION

TO STARE WOULD BE IMPOLITE
TO BRAKE WOULD BE AN OBVIOUS OVERSIGHT

YOU SLOW JUST ENOUGH TO CONNECT BY SIGHT
BUT THE CRACKED VIEW-SPACE IS NEARLY AIR-TIGHT

OH NO...CAN'T STOP THAT FEELING
IT'S JUST SO DAMN APPEALING
ATTEMPTS TO SUPPRESS IT WILL SURELY FAIL
IT ALWAYS RETURNS TO THE SENDER LIKE MISLABELED MAIL

YOU ONLY SEE THE BRIM OF HER HAT
BUT YOU IMAGINE THE POINTS OF INTEREST ON HER MAP

YOUR THOUGHTS SOON WANDER AS THE AUTO NOW SWAYS
YOU THINK TO YOURSELF IS SHE THE FALL TO MY SUMMER DAYS

AWAKENED BY THE SOUND OF A PASSING CADILLAC
SHE EXITS YOUR HIGHWAY AS YOU EASE THE SEAT BACK…THAT IS THAT

YOU'VE LOST THAT FEELING
IT DOESN'T ALWAYS FEEL LIKE STEALING
YOU SAY YOUR NEEDS NEED HEALING…
YOU BETTER GET KNEELING

RESET

I NEVER WANT TO VACATION WITHOUT YOU
NEVER WANT TO BE OUT-OF-REACH FROM RESCUE

YOU SEE, YOUR LINES…THEY BORDER ME
YOUR LIPS…COLOR MY HEART INCANDESCENTLY

YOU'RE ALWAYS THE LAST SENTENCE ON THE PAGE OF MY BOOK
…A GEMSTONE POLISHED BY A CLEAR-WATER BROOK

YOU'RE MY RESET BUTTON…THE ONE I PRESS SO OFTEN
A RAINDROP ON MY DRY SKIN…MOISTURE TO SOFTEN
WITH ONE WORD YOU CAN ERASE THE WRONG
WITH ONE GLANCE YOU CAN AGAIN MAKE ME STRONG

OH…YOU SAMPLE ME LIKE A BOX OF CHOCOLATE
THE TASTE OF YOU…THERE IS NO WAY I COULD EVER FORGET

TIME SEEMS TO STRETCH WHEN I AM ABSENT FROM YOUR FOLD
CAN I EVER REPAY YOUR KIND GIFTS OF GOLD

YOU'RE THE STRENGTH IN MY ARMS AND THE VEINS TO MY WRIST
A POISON-IVY ITCH WITH MY HEART CLUTCHED FIRMLY BY YOUR FIST

YOU'RE MY RESET BUTTON…NO MORE FLASHING RED LIGHTS
YOUR LOVE…IT PAINTS THE SKY ON DARKENED NIGHTS
COVER ME WITH THE WARMTH OF A CAMP-FIRE
LIFT MY SOUL…FILL ME WITH DEEPENED DESIRE

A CINNAMON SEA, YOUR WATERS CONTINUE TO CARRY ME
SPUN AS IF A TOY-TOP, I SOMETIMES LEAN BUT YOU NEVER LET ME DROP

THE ICE AND SNOW USED TO WEIGH HEAVY AGAINST MY WALLS
THE SUN IN YOUR EYES NOW MELTS THOSE HARDENED YEARS INTO WATERFALLS

THE WIND CAN'T PUSH MY FLIGHT HIGHER THAN YOU
EVEN THE ANGELS ALL BELIEVE THAT YOUR WINGS ARE OVERDUE

YOU'RE MY RESET BUTTON…A CASINO WHICH CASHES MY CHIPS
…THE TASTE OF SALT NO LONGER SEASONS MY LIPS
I WANT YOU TO BE MY PILLOW AND MY PLATFORM
MY PULSE, MY PARENT, MY PROTECTION IN THE STORM

LYRICS

(NEGATIVE)

IN THIS POOL

A BIG APPETITE, BUT YOU HAVE NO FORK OR KNIFE
THEY FILL YOUR BELLY WITH WARM GOO,...A PHONY LIFE

A FEELING OF COMFORT WITHOUT SUBSTANCE IS NOW FELT
GREATNESS WORN RATHER MEEKLY IS IN NEED OF A BELT

IN THIS POOL YOU SWIM TO THE DEEP-END...
KNOWING YOUR INSECURITIES YOU USUALLY PRETEND
IN THIS POOL THE WATER IS FAR FROM STILL
ALCOHOL FIGHTS THE BOREDOM, BUT THE HEADACHES...NOW YOUR WILL

IT'S UNBELIEVABLE THE THINGS YOU WANT, NEED AND DO...
THE SPOOL OF THREAD UNWOUND, A NEEDLE RIPPING THROUGH

HEAVY IS THE WORLD, BUT LIGHT IS THE DISCIPLINE OF FATE
LIFE IS A SERIES OF POCKETS, DEEP AND WADED, TO FILL OR VACATE

IN THIS POOL THE LANE MARKERS WIDEN
HEY BIRD THE WORM WANTS YOU TO JUST SLIDE IN
IN THIS POOL THE WATER IS SALTY-THICK
YOUR HEAD BARELY ABOVE, YOUR FEET TIED TO A BRICK

YOUR LIPS SPEAK A LANGUAGE OF WHICH I'M NOT ACQUAINTED
YOU USE MORE COLOR IN EMOTION THAN DAVINCCI PAINTED

YOU CAN'T PUT A NET OVER INSPIRATION, IT WILL CHEW RIGHT THROUGH
AND YOU CAN'T STOP A CAR WITH A WHITE-PAINT-LINE OR GUARDRAIL VIEW

IN THIS POOL THE ODDS ARE GREATLY SWAYED
NUMBERS LIKE CYMBALS, FREQUENTLY PLAYED
IN THIS POOL THE MONEY NEVER WASHES CLEAN
IN THIS POOL…YOU LIKE IT DIRTY AND ROUTINE

TENDER-HEART (2)

BUSINESS-LIKE, YOU FLIP ME LIKE PAGES IN A MAG
A HARLEY BIKE, YOU CHANGE GEARS AND START TO DRAG

MY MIND IS STEAMED BY A TEMPERED THOUGHT…
I CAN'T SEE YOU ANY MORE AND MY HELPING HAND IS CAUGHT

DRIVE…YEAH I GUESS YOU GOT WHAT IT TAKES
SURVIVE…DO WHATEVER TO ESCAPE THE SNAKES
TENDER-HEART YOU USE TO SURRENDER
TENDER-HEART WILL YOU EVER REMEMBER

YOU SEE YOU'RE DROWNING AND I CAN'T SAVE YOU
CUTTING, THE LIGHT REVEALS YOUR THIN RESIDUE

WHAT ONCE WAS FIRE NOW SPARKS REGRET
PAST WATER SPILLS OVER THE BRIDGE VERY UPSET

I LIKE TO STAY SHARP, YOU MAKE ME BLUNT
YOU'RE A MOVIE-DOUBLE WHO'S LIFE IS A STUNT
TENDER-HEART YOU USE TO HAVE PASSION
TENDER-HEART WHY DO YOU DASH AND RUN

PEOPLE COVER THEIR BRAKES WHEN YOU PASS
A ROCK IN THE ROAD YOU MAKE CARS CRASH

SPRINGBOARD-LOVE WITH NO POOL TO LAND IN
YOU KEEP ON PUSHING TOWARD AN UNPLANNED WIN

I'VE LOST THAT NEW CAR FEELING…MY SWEET
JUST A BALLOON HITTING THE CEILING…BEAT
TENDER-HEART YOU USE TO CARE SO MUCH
TENDER-HEART WHAT HAPPENED TO THAT TENDER TOUCH

DIZZYING HEIGHTS

UNCERTAINTY STITCHES YOUR WARDROBE
NOTHING ON THE SURFACE…SO YOU PROBE

YOU DRIVE YOURSELF WITH A SOFT SHOE
NEVER IN TUNE WITH A DETAILED VIEW…

YOU'RE REACHING DIZZYING HEIGHTS
UP SO HIGH THAT YOU HAVE NO TRAFFIC LIGHTS
BOATS AND PLANES, PILLS FOR THE RICH
YOUR APPETITE CRAVES A BIG CASH SANDWICH

YOU BOX ME, THAT'S RIGHT…LEFT THEN UPPERCUT
AND THOSE DOORS OF HOLINESS ARE CLOSED SHUT

I KNOW ALL OF YOUR TELLTALE ANXIETIES…
DADDY'S LITTLE GIRL, SO HARD TO PLEASE

YOU'RE REACHING DIZZYING HEIGHTS
YOU SAY THAT YOU NEED TO SEE NEW SIGHTS
USING YOUR GOD-GIFTS TO CLIMB AND PERCH
DOWN THE FELLOW-BRICK ROAD GOES YOUR SEARCH

YOU TAUGHT ME HOW TO STAND SLEEPING…
NOW I'M CAUGHT BETWEEN LOVE'S-THROWAWAY AND KEEPING

THERE IS ALWAYS MORE WEIGHT ON YOUR DOWN-STROKE
AND YOU STEADILY GIVE OXYGEN TO FIRES THAT SMOKE

YOU'RE REACHING DIZZYING HEIGHTS
…NOSE BLEEDS WITHOUT FISTFIGHTS
ASCENDING IN A DESCENDING FASHION
REACHING DIZZYING HEIGHTS HAS BECOME YOUR PASSION

A LETTER NEVER MAILED

YOU SAID YOU HATED ME…
YOU SAID YOU SHOULD HAVE NEVER LET YOURSELF SEE
ALL IN A LETTER THAT YOU NEVER MAILED

YOU SAY THAT LIFE IS JUST STOP-SIGNS AND RAILROAD CROSSINGS
AND LOVE IS THE PURCHASE THAT OFTEN KEEPS ON COSTING
ALL IN A LETTER THAT YOU NEVER MAILED

YOU WANT A LIFE THAT EVOLVES AROUND YOU
YOU NEED THE COMFORT OF MONEY AND SECURITY TOO
ALL IN A LETTER THAT YOU NEVER MAILED

WITH PEN AND PAPER YOU WENT FOR THE HEART
YOU TRIED TO REWRITE THE SCRIPT WITH A BRAND NEW PART
CARING, WAS IT REALLY THE BOAT THAT NEVER SAILED
ALL IN A LETTER THAT YOU NEVER MAILED

YOU CLAIM THERE ARE NO GIVERS ON THIS EARTH
YOU BELIEVE NO ONE KNOWS YOUR TRUE WORTH
ALL IN A LETTER THAT YOU NEVER MAILED

YOU BARELY BEND AND YOU NEVER BREAK
YOU'LL BE DAMNED IF ANY ONE EVER RIDE'S YOUR WAKE
ALL IN A LETTER THAT YOU NEVER MAILED

YOU SAY THE ASPIRIN ONLY QUIETS THE PAIN
YOU SAY THE CLOUDS ONLY BLOCK THE SUNSHINE WITH RAIN
ALL IN A LETTER THAT YOU NEVER MAILED

YOU THINK IT'S ALL SUCH A BIG DISAPPOINTMENT
BUT YOU NEVER REALLY ADDRESSED THE PAST TIMES SPENT
WAS SATISFACTION ALWAYS HIDDEN, NEVER UNVEILED
ALL IN A LETTER THAT YOU NEVER MAILED

YOU WONDER, ARE THERE THINGS THAT YOU'RE MISSING
YOU SPEND YOUR HOURS OFTEN GOOD-TIME REMINISCING
ALL IN A LETTER THAT YOU NEVER MAILED

YOU WILL ALWAYS TRADE HAPPINESS FOR SILVER AND GOLD
WILL HOPE EVER FAVOR YOUR FAULTS AS YOU GROW OLD
ALL IN A LETTER THAT YOU NEVER MAILED

YOUR WINDOWS WERE ALWAYS TINTED BLACK
YOU'RE A BUTTERFLY WITH A HIDDEN TENDENCY TO ATTACK
ALL IN A LETTER THAT YOU NEVER MAILED

IT'S HARD TO BE CUT WHEN YOU NEVER BLEED
YOU'RE A PLANT WHOSE FLOWERS CARRY THE DEADLIEST SEED
WAS OUR TRAIN EVER MOVING WHEN IT EVENTUALLY DERAILED
ALL IN A LETTER THAT YOU NEVER MAILED

MERCY

SINNED IN CHICAGO,…GOT SUNBURNED ON MY BACK
PINNED LIKE CARGO INSIDE A TRUCK, MY PROBLEMS SLOWLY STACK

I KILL MY BODY ON THE WEEKEND, PUT IT BACK TOGETHER THE OTHER FIVE
I TRIED TO HEAL MYSELF IN YOU, BUT THE FIRE AND HEAT DIDN'T SURVIVE

IF MERCY WAS A SUDDEN FALL, I WOULDN'T LOSE ANY BLOOD
JESUS…WHAT WENT WRONG WITH ME, MY LIFE IS ANCHORED IN MUD
MERCY, A PLACE I USED TO BE DURING HOLIDAY…
NOW I JUST SINK TO THE GROUND AND CRAWL AWAY

LOVE'S-DISAPPOINTMENT,…STORM CLOUDS, LIGHTNING…RAIN
HEADLIGHTS AND HEADACHES, TRY TO SHINE WITHOUT PAIN

EVERYONE KNOWS MR. TEMPTATION, BUT DOES HE SIT AT THE TABLE
SOMETIMES SELF-ACCREDITATION IS SERVED,…RESISTANCE WHEN ABLE

IF MERCY WAS MONEY, MY PENNIES WOULDN'T SUM TEN CENTS
SOMETIMES WOOD MUST BE SPLINTERED FROM THE SURROUNDING FENCE
MERCY, A NAME I GIVE TO THE LOST ADDRESS IN MY HEAD
MY BLACK-BOOK, NOW A FISH HOOK, WATCHES THE SHARKS GET FED

THINGS WANTED AND THINGS GAINED, YOUR TIMING CAN SLIP
COLLAPSED LEFTOVERS WRAPPED IN CELLOPHANE…STAR-TING TO RIP

I AM EMOTIONALLY BROKE AND NOW IN-DEBT TO DECEIT…
SOMETHING OF A NOTHING-DAY, I'VE BEEN SOFTENED BY THIS DEFEAT

IF MERCY COULD BE MADE, I'D SUGAR THE LEMONADE
I WOULD WANT TO FREEZE IT, SAVE IT FOR ANOTHER DAY
MERCY, THIS ACTION IS ONE OF HIGH PROFILE…
MERCY, MY SPIRIT NEEDS CALM AND COMFORT FOR AWHILE

THE AMOUNT OF YOUR SOUL

YOU'VE MADE YOUR BED, BUT THE PILLOWS STILL SMOTHER
IDEAS THAT WERE ONCE BELIEFS NOW BATTLE EACH OTHER

YOUR SPIRIT'S ACCENT HAS HAD AN ACCIDENT…
TRIPPED, YOU'RE NOW FALLING TO THE PAVEMENT

WHAT'S IT ALL COME DOWN TO…
YOUR WANTS, THEY LEAVE A THIN RESIDUE
THE WATERMARK ONLY HITS HALF OF THE POLE
DOLLARS OR DIMES…. THE AMOUNT OF YOUR SOUL

OH HOW YOU THOUGHT YOU HAD PROTECTION, EVEN LEVERAGE
…INSTEAD, AN INFECTION AND A WATERED-DOWN BEVERAGE

A GLANCE AT THE PAST REVEALS A VERY THIN SHIELD
CAN YOUR HARVEST LAST OR SHOULD YOU PLANT A NEW FIELD

THE STAIRWAY YOU CLIMB LEADS TO AN EMPTY TOWER
AND YOUR CONSCIENCE BEGINS TO SWELL WITH FALSE POWER
YOU GRASP TIGHTEST THE THINGS WITH NO CONTROL
GRAY OR GOLD…THE AMOUNT OF YOUR SOUL

SMALL IS THE TABLE AT WHICH YOU DINE
YOUR KNIFE DULL AS IT CUTS THE SUBLIME

IF A POINT ON A COMPASS, YOUR HEART WOULD SHOW SOUTH
THE THOUGHTS IN YOUR HEAD NOW STICK IN YOUR MOUTH

YOUR FOUNDATION IS MADE OF FORTUNES LOST
AND YOUR DREAMS…WAVES ON WHICH YOUR ARE TOSSED
ENERGIES EXTENDED THROUGH TEMPTATION AND TOLL
FABLE OR PAPAL…THE AMOUNT OF YOUR SOUL

BEVELED

YOU RISE LIKE STEAM AND BURN OFTEN
YET YOU SELDOM SEEM TO BEND OR SOFTEN

YOUR SIGHT, A VIEWING OF WHAT USED TO BE…
YOU HANDS, STEALING GOLD FROM OUR TREASURY

BEVELED…DID THE FEELING LEAVE YOUR BONES
BETTER CALL ELVIS AND JESUS ON THEIR CELL PHONES
BEVELED, LOSING YOUR FOOTING EVERY DAY
ROAD-BLOCKS NOT HURDLED JUST STAY IN YOUR WAY

LAVENDER A FAVORITE OF YOURS…COLOR AND MOOD
A HEAD FLIP OR A SWINGING HIP, IT'S ALL JUST ATTITUDE

MY DAYS END WITH A DRINK POURED FROM MOUNT GIN
IN LOVE'S PRESENCE YOU SWIM A RIVER, BUT NEVER DIVE IN

BEVELED, YOUR RESTRAINT IS LIKE SPILLED WATER ON A TILE FLOOR
YOUR ANGER…GARBAGE,…HOLES IN THE STOCKINGS YOU ONCE WORE
BEVELED, WITH A WRENCH-SET YOU LOVE TO TWIST AND TURN…
ALL THAT GLITTERS…SHINES IN YOUR EYES AND BEGINS TO BURN

LOOK HOW THE CAUSE NOW JUDGES THE EFFECT…
UNDER THE MOONLIGHT OF LESSER THINGS YOU TRY TO PROTECT

WASN'T LOVE MEANT TO BATHE US AT CLOUD-LEVEL…
INSTEAD HEAVEN'S UPSIDE-DOWN AND YOU'RE THE DEVIL

BEVELED, STALE AIR ON THE PLANE YOU'RE FLYING
I JUMP RATHER THAN LAND ON THE GROUND…DYING
BEVELED, NOW WHAT DID GOD DROP INTO YOUR LAP
SOMETIMES KISSES AND HUGS FALL OFF OF THE MAP

BLURRED VISION

HER VOICE SOUNDS LIKE A ROCK HITTING TIN
HER JUDGMENT, A MISTAKE THAT SHE'S DROWNING IN

SHE COLORS HER HAIR TO HIDE THE HINT OF HURT
SHE TRIES TO BUILD A FRAMEWORK FROM NOTHING BUT DIRT

BLURRED VISION...
HER EYES CAN'T READ THE BRICK WALL
BLURRED VISION...
INDECISION, BOTH THE ENTRANCE AND THE EXIT CALL

SHE DIVERTS HER ATTENTION TO A DIFFERENT VIEW...
FOR WHAT PASSES HER EYES ARE LIES,...DISAPPOINTMENT TOO

A SOUR TASTE ON THE TONGUE OF BLISS...
SHE TRIES TO PURGE THE PAST WITH A HUG AND A KISS

BLURRED VISION...
WHAT WAS ONCE SEEN HAS NOW FADED BLACK
BLURRED VISION...
A ONCE ALLY HAS TURNED IN HASTE TO ATTACK

SHE STAYS, MAYBE HIS ACTIONS WILL VARY
HER HAZE, A PAGE IN A FICTION-BOOK...SCARY

EDDIE, SHE CAN'T FIND A BETTER MAN...
SHE'S CRYING AND CRAWLING, DYING WHILE FALLING...
A SPRINTER THAT NEVER RAN

BLURRED VISION...
A MIST OF PAIN AND JOY VAPOR-MIXED
BLURRED VISION...
A BROKEN WINDOW WITH GLASS IN HAND, UNFIXED

THE REST OF YOUR LOVE

SLOWLY WE TOUCH…
BUT YOU SAY NOT TOO MUCH
SIMPLE THINGS DON'T ALWAYS APPEAR THAT WAY…
WHEN YOU'RE PRISON-BOUND…YOU WEAR PRISON-GRAY

YOU BRING TO THE TABLE THE TASTE FOR HABIT
…AND CAN ONLY FEAST UPON COLOR IF YOU STAB IT
YOUR HEART'S AN APARTMENT WITH WEAK CEILINGS ABOVE…
PLEASE LET ME FIND THE REST OF YOUR LOVE

WHAT DISAPPEARED IN THE DARK IS NOW CONSIDERED LOST
BUT A LIGHT NOW SHINES UPON A THINNING FROST
A BREATH CAN BE BREATHED INTO ONE'S SILENT CHEST
AND WARMTH CAN BE REGAINED THROUGH TENDERNESS

YOUR HEAD HAS DISABLED PAST MEMORY CHIPS
…AND YOUR TEETH LAY BEHIND THOSE CURTAINED LIPS
IN THE MIRROR YOU SQUINT TO SEE THE ONCE LIKENESS OF…
I WAIT TO FIND THE REST OF YOUR LOVE

CAN A SECTION OF HIGHWAY ABANDON ALL CONTACT
CAN A WAR BE WON WITHOUT A PLANNED ATTACK
LISTEN TO ME WHEN I EXPLAIN MY PRESENT CONCERN
I ONCE SLEPT IN THE COLD AND ONCE FEVERED THE BURN

NEVER A HUNDRED, MAYBE SEVENTY OR EIGHTY PERCENT…
SUCH A MYSTERY OR SECRET WHERE THOSE LOST FEELINGS WENT
IT MUST HAVE BEEN THE FIGHT THAT CAUSED YOU TO SHOVE…
I DUCK TO FIND THE REST OF YOUR LOVE

SINKING

SHE'S A RAZOR BLADE...
CUTTING WITHOUT FIRST-AID

SHE NEVER KNEW HOW MUCH OF AN EDGE SHE WORE
IT SEEMS HER ONLY PRIORITY WAS GETTING MORE

PREVIOUSLY STAINED BY ANOTHER MAN, SHE NOW STANDS OPEN AND HOL-
LOW
NEVER REALLY TAKING LOVE'S HAND, SHE WILL FOREVER CHASE AND FOLLOW

I NEVER DID LIKE THAT SINKING FEELING
THAT PAIN OF SOMEONE HEART-STEALING
THAT CUT WHEN LOVE'S SURGERY BEGINS
THAT DEVIL DISGUISED IN SHEEP SKINS

SHE MUST BE BLIND, SHE ALWAYS SWINGS TWICE AT HER MARK
CHECKS HER FACE IN THE REFLECTION OF YOUR CAR WHILE DARK

YOU CAN'T CHANGE THE COURSE OF A BURIED SHIP
AND YOU CAN'T TASTE THE BLOOD AS SHE BITES YOUR BOTTOM LIP

NEVER KNOWING THE DIRECTION SHE WILL FALL
SHE HAS NO NETS TO CATCH THE WEIGHT OF HER CRUMBLING WALL

I NEVER DID LIKE THAT SINKING FEELING
EMOTIONS COUNTER-CLOCKWISE REELING
TEARS ON THE WINDSHIELD SOULDN'T CAUSE CONCERN
...WHEN WILL SHE EVER LEARN

HER SKIN HAS NO TIME TO REWIND YOU NEW
REMEMBER, THE SOUL OF A SIREN IS SMALL AND THICK-FILLED WITH GLUE

TANNED SKIN BUT A FADED INNER STAR
HER ATTITUDE SLIPS FROM SWIGS TO SIPS IN THIS EMOTIONAL BAR

SHE'S THE HAND THAT STIRS THE WITCHES BREW
...A FOLD IN THE GOWN THAT MEDUSSA GAVE FORM TO

I NEVER DID LIKE THAT SINKING FEELING
WHEN YOUR SOUL HAS BEEN FORCED TO KEEP KNEELING
SEEMS I'M ALWAYS POKER DEALING...
HER CONSCIOUSNESS I'M CONVINCED HAS NO MORAL CEILING

SOUTH AND NORTH

ONE MINUTE I'M TOUCHING YOUR HAND
WITHIN SECONDS I'M SINKING IN SAND

IT'S NOT THE ABUNDANCE OF LOVE...IT'S THE TEMPERATURE
IT'S NOT THE BELIEF IN HEAVEN ABOVE, IT'S THE ACT OF BEING SURE

I REMEMBER WHEN I USE TO LEASE SPACE IN YOUR HEART
BUT YOUR RENT WENT UP, THE WALLS GREW TALL AND THEN THE SPACE GREW
DARK

LIKE FINGERNAILS CUT TOO SHORT
LIKE THE BIBLE ON THE WITNESS STAND IN COURT
YOU'RE BACK AND FORTH
...SOUTH AND NORTH

I MISS OUR CONVERSATIONS LATELY
I MISS MY MIND'S EASE...WEIGHT-FREE

LOST VISIONS OF VICTORY...
WHERE IS THAT ODOR OF SWEET SIMPLICITY

LIKE A TIDE THAT FLOWS IN, YOU SWIFTLY ROLL OUT
YOU ALWAYS GIVE ME QUARTER'S-ODDS WHEN I'M TOSSED ABOUT

COFFEE-CUP LOVE, SOMETIMES CREAM...SOMETIMES BLACK
SOMETIMES I STAY OVER, SOMETIMES I DON'T EVEN UNPACK
HAS OUR LOVE RUN ITS COURSE...
YOU'RE SOUTH AND NORTH

YOU TEND TO DART THEN WEAVE...AND OFTEN LEAVE
WITH YOUR INCONSISTENCIES WHAT DO YOU HOPE TO ACHIEVE

SIMPLE UNDERSTANDINGS MET WITH GEOGRAPHIC DIVIDE
FEELINGS THAT ARE NEVER DEMANDING BUT COUPLED WITH PRIDE

WILL WE EVER RETURN TO OUR HOME'S FRONT GATE
WILL THE RIP I FEEL BE TORN COMPLETELY OR RETURN TO ITS PRIOR STATE

AM I JUST THE HOOD-EMBLEM ON YOUR CAR
A CANDY-WRAPPER TO YOUR CHOCOLATE BAR
COOL MOONLIGHT OR A SUNLIGHT SCORCH
YOU'RE SOUTH AND NORTH

GUNS DRAWN

MY CAR NO LONGER PROTECTS ME FROM SHARKS' TEETH AND SABERS
THEY BEAT ME DOWN, BURN MY SKIN…ALL FOR THE SPOILS OF MY LABORS

SO MANY TRY TO TAKE THE COALS WHICH POWER MY SUN
PLEASE TELL ME LORD I'M NOT THE ONLY CONSCIOUS ONE

OVER-WORKED COGS AND RUSTED WHEELS
MY BRAIN SOMETIMES NO LONGER FEELS

SLOWER MOVES
DEEPENED GROVES
SEASIDE DAWN
GUNS DRAWN

MY SHIELD IS RAISED BUT MY BREAST-PLATE IS REMOVED
THE CROWN TO MY KINGDOM SLIPS INTO MY SKIN FOR A TIGHTER GROOVE

SO MANY BATTLES WHICH LED TO THIS WAR
COMPETITION EFFECTS HOW WE BREATHE AS MY STOMACH SINKS TO THE
FLOOR

I'LL NEVER BE A PRISON GUARD…NO CAPTIVES IN MY TENTS
TO LIVE IS NOT TO COMMAND, TO GIVE ORDERS JUST DOESN'T MAKE ANY SENSE

MONEY, IT ISN'T WORTH THE EXPENSE
PLEASE…HOLD ALL GUILTY COMMENTS
TO MOVE FORWARD THEY SAY YOU NEED BRAWN
GUNS DRAWN

IS THERE A BULLET COLORED BY MY FAMILY CREST
ARE THE WORDS HONOR AND GLORY INSCRIBED ON MY CHEST

THOUGHTS TODAY DON'T SURPASS THOSE THAT ALREADY EXIST
FEARFUL…AM I THE LAST ONE TO GO OR AM I FIRST ON THEIR LIST

EMOTIONAL GRAVES...ALREADY DEEPLY MINED
THE ROPES THAT TIE...WILL THEY FOREVER BIND

GOD WANTS YOU TO BE KIND
THE WORLD NEEDS YOU TO REMAIN BLIND
MIDDLE-BOUND, YOU CONTINUE TO YAWN
GUNS DRAWN

DIDN'T YOU

WHEN YOU RUB YOUR EYES…DO THE VISIONS CLEAR
DRINKS AFTER WORK WILL MAKE THE SPIRITS REAPPEAR

FREEDOM'S PRICE IS A PAYCHECK AWAY
IF YOU WALK THE LINE ALL OF THE TIME…CAN YOU EVER STRAY

FAMILY WISHES AND WANTS, BACK-HAND SERVICE YOU'RE QUICK TO RETURN
TOO BAD THOSE BLOCKS OF TIME ARE USED TO BUILD WALLS THAT OFTEN
BURN

DIDN'T YOU KNOW THE WORLD LIKES TO KEEP NEAT PILES
WHITE-PRESSED SHIRTS, WAXED CARS AND ALL SURGICAL SMILES
OFTEN STROKED BY FINGERS TO CALLOUS TO FEEL
LIFTING AND MOVING DIRT CAN BECOME A THIRSTY ORDEAL

YOU'RE MUCH WORSE-OFF THAN YOU PRETEND TO LOOK
SOMETIMES A SET MIND CAN AND WILL BE SUDDENLY SHOOK

CERTAIN COURAGE ONLY APPEARS AT DETERMINED TIMES
ONE NEVER KNOWS WHEN THEY'LL COMMIT MORE DUMB-CRIMES

I'LL KEEP PLAYING THE LOTTERY…JUST LIKE YOU
WE ALL NEED SOME FORTUNES TO FALL INTO

DIDN'T YOU KNOW THAT THE STATUES CAN SPEAK
THEY UPLIFT THE STRONG AND PARENT THE WEAK
BUT YOU PRETEND NOT TO HEAR AND FAIL TO HEED
YOU WON'T EVER STOP DYING IF YOU CONTINUE TO BLEED

YOU SAY TO FINISH FATE IT WILL REQUIRE A SHOTGUN BLAST
THE CHAIR'S RECLINED, YOU STEAL SIPS OF MY DRINK…BUT SWALLOW NONE
TOO FAST

THE CALENDAR DAYS NEVER ASK IF THEY CAN ADVANCE
THUMB-TACK FEELINGS, POCKET-HIDDEN…REMAIN LEFT TO CHANCE

REPOSSESSING FEELINGS ONLY TO THROW THEM BACK AGAIN
DO YOU LIKE SIGNING YOUR CHECKS WITH AN EMPTY INKPEN

DIDN'T YOU KNOW WE ALL FEEL THE PAIN
THAT NEED TO CLEANSE A HARDENED, STUBBORN STAIN
JUST TRY TO TUNNEL TO THE OTHER SIDE…THEN BACK
LEAVE YOUR ARMY BEHIND BUT REMEMBER TO BRING A PLANNED ATTACK

D.L.G.

SHE'LL WAIVE THE SWORD OF PAIN, IF DADDY SAYS DO IT AGAIN
SHE'LL BREAK YOU IN TWO THEN LEAVE YOU…DRAINED

SHE'S ALWAYS RUNNING BECAUSE IT HURTS TO STAND STILL
SO MANY WRONGS, MEMORIES THAT BRUISE…DADDY'S ILL

DADDY'S LITTLE GIRL WANTS TO PLEASE
SHE WANTS TO CURE DADDY'S DISEASE
DADDY'S LITTLE GIRL…NEVER ALLOWED TO GROW UP
HER MOUTH WAS FORCED TO DRINK FROM DADDY'S CUP

CERTAIN EVENTS…A SOAP OPERA YOU CAN'T FIND ON TV
HE NEVER HAD TO GIVE LOVE…ONLY GAIN SYMPATHY

FOR POP SHE'LL SWALLOW A NIGHTMARE AND CAST-OUT A DREAM
FOR POP SHE'LL SLEEP WITH THE DEVIL JUST TO MEND THE SEAM

DADDY'S LITTLE GIRL LIVES FOR THE YES NOD
APPROVAL FROM PAPA IS LIKE A BLESSING FROM GOD
DADDY'S LITTLE GIRL WILL PASS DESIRE TO THE MONEY PLATE
DADDY CONTROLS THOUGHTS WITH THREATS…DARK DECEIVING BAIT

IN HER MIND THE SPEACHES RUN ON A CONSTANT LOOP
WILL SHE EVER SPEAK THE WORDS YELLED BY HER FOREHEAD GROUP

IT'S A TIME-BOMB LOVE, TICK TOCK…BOOM
SHE SITS ALONE WITHIN THE DARKNESS WE CALL DOOM

DADDY'S LITTLE GIRL, CONSCIENCE FAR FROM THE SURFACE
BUT INDEPENDENCE IS RISING…RIDING HOPE'S HAPPINESS
DADDY'S LITTE GIRL, ALWAYS SWIMMING THROUGH THE BOG
DLG HAS A MAN IN THE DISTANCE WITH SOUL-MATE DIALOGUE

DOWN-ANGEL

YOU'RE A DEVIL, A DEFINITE STEP TO A LOWER LEVEL
A BAR-CODE-BARGAIN, A DEFINITE DISCOUNT, OVER-PRICED AT ANY AMOUNT

WHY DID YOU TRY TO SHARPEN YOUR HORNS ON ME
DIDN'T YOU KNOW I'M HALO-BLESSED AND TEMPTATION FREE

YET YOU STILL TRIED TO BURN ME WITH YOUR FULL-TIME FIRES
…TRIED TO TURN MY HEART'S PRISON GUARDS INTO FEEBLE LIARS

ANGEL IN DISGUISE…
YOU WANT TO BE EVERYONE'S PRIZE
WHERE ARE THOSE WINGS YOU USED TO OWN
WHEN DID YOU FALL, WHEN DID THE LIGHT DIM ON THOSE THINGS ONCE SHOWN

YOUR TAIL, ALL-DIRECTION-POINTED
AND YOUR KINGDOM IS CERTAINLY SELF-ANOINTED

HOW LONG HAVE YOU BEEN THIS WAY
DID YOU REALLY BELIEVE THAT I WOULD STAY

YOU COLLECT SOULS LIKE STAMPS OR DOLLS
YOUR NEED FOR BLOOD IS A HUNGER BURIED DEEP WITHIN YOUR BOWELS

ANGEL IN DISGUISE…
DON'T YOU KNOW THAT ALL THE RULES APPLY
YOU CAN'T LEAP IF YOU CAN'T FLY…
IS YOUR HEART BLACKED BY THE LIGHT-RAY SKY

SEASONED BY SORROW YOUR TEMPERATURE AND TEMPER RUN HOT
IT SEEMS TO ME YOU'RE ALWAYS TRYING TO BECOME SOMETHING YOU'RE NOT

WITH YOUR HAIR OF SNAKES AND TONGUE OF TOXIN
YOU ATTEMPT TO BITE THE NECKS OF THOSE BOXED-IN

WILL YOU EVER STOP, WILL YOU APPETITE EVER REACH ITS END
WILL YOU EVER LET ME HELP, LET LOVE BECOME YOUR FRIEND

ANGEL IN DISGUISE…
WHAT'S REALLY BEHIND THOSE EYES
COME, BACK AWAY FROM THAT SKY-SCRAPED DROP
REJOIN ME AND PAST PURITY, JUST SAY WHEN TO STOP

FALLEN

SWEETNESS TURNS TO SOUR
AND KINDNESS LOSES ITS POWER
WHEN HAPPINESS FALLS DOWN

YOUR MIND STARTS TO PRETEND
AND THE DAYS NEVER END
WHEN HAPPINESS FALLS DOWN

WHEN HAPPINESS FALLS DOWN
YOUR KNEES SCRAPE THE GROUND
ENDLESS SLEEP TO HELP SUB-SET THE GRIEF
SHOULD REALITY EVER BECOME A PRACTICED BELIEF

YOUR DREAMS HALF-CUT BEGIN TO BLEED
AND YOUR HEART WILL NO LONGER FEED
WHEN HAPPINESS FALLS DOWN

YOUR CLOTHES CAN'T CHANGE THIS CIRCUMSTANCE
AND LOVE'S SONG WON'T PERMIT YOU TO DANCE
WHEN HAPPINESS FALLS DOWN

WHEN HAPPINESS FALLS DOWN
THE GREEN-TREE LEAVES TURN BROWN
THE SKY AND SUN FADE BLACK
EMPTINESS NO LONGER WITHDRAWS WITHOUT AN ATTACK

YOUR ROADS ARE CRUSHED BY AN UNSEEN FORCE
AND THE DEVIL IS NOW THE JOCKEY ON YOUR THOROUGHBRED HORSE
WHEN HAPPINESS FALLS DOWN

EVERY JOB AND TASK…A BURDEN
WHEN THE FEELING IN YOUR GUT BECOMES CERTAIN
…THAT'S HAPPINESS FALLING DOWN

WHEN HAPPINESS FALLS DOWN
…DOES IT EVER REALLY MAKE AN OUTSIDE SOUND
IS IT ABOUT KEEPING EMOTIONS UNDER CONTROL
OR IS IT ALL JUST ABOUT RESETTING, REPLANTING YOUR SOUL

BLACK FAITH

MAINTAINING YOUR LINE BETWEEN SASS AND COOL
YOU LET SOMEONE ELSE DO THE WORK FOR YOU

ONE TO NEVER WORRY ABOUT WHAT HAPPENS NEXT
YOU PROCESS SOCIAL EVENTS LIKE READING PRE-SCHOOL TEXT

THE OUTER EDGE YOU WALK IS A VERY THIN ROPE
WHEN YOU'RE DOWN, EMPTY FEELINGS DANCE WITH THE DICE TO COPE

CHANGE YOUR BLACK FAITH, SAVE YOUR SOUL
REMEMBER THAT CHILD WHICH MADE YOU WHOLE
TAG YOUR FEELINGS LIKE A TRAVEL-SUITCASE…
HEAL THE BROKEN BONES WITH A TIGHTENED BRACE

A PIÑATA HEART, ONE MORE HIT AND IT WILL BREAK APART
THIEVERY BY BELIEVABILITY IS SUCH A LOST ART

COCKY S.O.B…HARDENED STEEL-ARMOR NATURALLY
BI-POLAR MOUNTAINS THAT WHICH YOU'VE LEARNED TO SOMEHOW SKI

YOU'RE A CROW THAT STANDS IN HIGHWAY TRAFFIC…TAUNTING CARS
SHADOWED LIGHT, AN IMPRESSIVE SIGHT, ABLE TO HEAL QUICKLY WITHOUT
SCARS

CHANGE YOUR BLACK FAITH, SAVE YOUR SOUL
RETURN THE REINS TO THE HORSE NAMED CONTROL
COME OUT OF THE DESERT WITHOUT THE TASTE FOR SAND
ASSIGN SOME TIME TO TOUCH THE SURFACE OF VISIONS UNPLANNED

…TAKE IN THE CRISP, CLEAN, COLD CITY AIR
TRY TO DESTROY THE THOUGHT THAT LOVE IS THE REFUSE OF DESPAIR

INSISTENT IS YOUR APPETITE FOR AN EMOTIONAL WARDROBE
ITS TASTE CHANGES WITH THE SPEED OF A FLASHING STROBE

HUNGRY FOR CHANGE, YOU SWALLOW SIN'S BRIDE-LESS' BULLET
IS EMPTINESS THE BEST WAY TO GAGE FEELINGS THAT AREN'T QUITE FULL YET

CHANGE YOUR BLACK FAITH, SAVE YOUR SOUL
KEEP ALL WHEELS DOWN, AVOID LOSS OF CONTROL
TOO MUCH CONFLICT WILL ALWAYS CAUSE GRAY-SMOKE
AS GASOLINE DESIRES THIRST FOR NEW REASONS TO CHOKE

REBUILT

TODAY'S THE DAY MY TRAIN RAN OFF THE TRACKS
PAST THOUGHTS DIE LIKE PASSENGERS WITH BROKEN NECKS

THIS TIME I'M GONNA BE BETTER THAN THE REST
VOICES INSIDE TELL ME THE TABLE IS FINALLY SET

YOU SEE I'M...
REBUILDING THE WALLS YOU KNOCKED DOWN
REBUILDING THE FEELINGS YOU BURIED UNDERGROUND
REBUILDING THE SUN INSIDE
REBUILDING THE LOVE THAT DIED

NO MORE STICKS AND STONES, NO MORE COMING UNDONE
ONCE CUT, NOW A CUT ABOVE...I AM SOMEONE

SOMETIMES YOU HAVE TO SWALLOW DIRT BEFORE YOU TASTE THE CLEAN
BETTER WASH YOUR MONEY IF YOU KNOW WHAT I MEAN

CAUSE' I'M...
REBUILDING THE MEMORIES I TRIED TO BURN
REBUILDING THE EVENTS YOU TRIED TO TURN
REBUILDING THAT FORGOTTEN SCENERY
REBUILDING WHO I USED TO BE

CAN'T TURN THIS FAUCET OFF, CAN ONLY BREAK THE CONTAINER
SPILLING SO MANY THOUGHTS I DROWNED MY ANGER

I'VE LEARNED SOMETIMES YOU GET DOWN, PULLED DOWN, TRAPPED IN A
ROOM
I DIDN'T LIKE THE HANDOUT...SO I GOT OUT, NOW WHAT ABOUT YOU

REBUILDING THE WALLS YOU KNOCKED DOWN
REBUILDING THE FEELINGS YOU BURIED UNDERGROUND
REBUILDING THE SUN INSIDE
REBUILDING THE LOVE THAT DIED

LOVE CHANGES

SO FILLED WITH POISON SHE NEEDS TO SPIT
SHE SITS BACK FOR PAYBACK READY TO HIT

SHE FALLS INTO USELESS BLACK
TRYING TO FIND THE DOORWAY BACK

THINGS THAT ONCE HELD HER UP NOW HOLD HER DOWN
LIFE CHANGES, NEW STAGES, OLD BUILDINGS BURNT TO THE GROUND

LOVE CHANGES EVERYTHING
CAN STRIP YOU OF ANYTHING
WILL TELL YOU IT'S ALL RIGHT
THEN LEAVE YOU IN THE NIGHT
LOVE CHANGES EVERYTHING

LONELINESS DOESN'T SHOW COLOR BUT SURE BLACKENS THE EYES
HEAD UNDERWATER HE'S PULLED DOWN WHERE THE SEDIMENT LIES

HE MISSES HER...BUT NOT ENOUGH TO CALL
BEEN PUSHED TO THE EDGE TOO MANY TIMES, HE BEGINS TO FALL

NO LONGER WILL EAT...HE'S BECOMING THIN-WAISTED
WHAT'S THIS NEW FLAVOR HE 'S TASTED

LOVE CHANGES EVERYTHING
CAN'T YOU FEEL THE STING
CUTS TAKE TIME TO HEAL
SCARS DON'T ALWAYS SEAL
WHEN LOVE CHANGES EVERYTHING

SOME DAY THEY WILL LIVE AGAIN
FIND ANOTHER TO REMOVE THE STAIN

SOMEONE WHO WILL FADE THEIR FEAR
SOMEONE WHO WON'T DISAPPEAR

LOVE CHANGES EVERYTHING
LISTEN TO THE BIRDS SING
NEWNESS FOUND
SPELLBOUND…
LOVE CHANGES EVERYTHING

BULLY LOVE

YOU SAY YOU'RE GONNA LEAVE ME…AS YOU RUN TO HIDE
YOU SAY YOU DON'T BELIEVE ME WHEN I TELL YOU WHAT I SEE INSIDE

SOMETIMES WHEN YOU MOVE I CAN ONLY SEE THE BLUR
MISSING SPACES ARE NEVER FILLED WHEN CONFIDENCE IS INSECURE

YES IT'S LOVE…
BULLY LOVE, FULLY LOVE
IT WILL COME AND KNOCK YOU DOWN
IT WILL SOMETIMES STAIN YOUR GOWN

YOU LIKE TO WRITE YOUR WORDS, LEAVING NOTES FOR ME
YOU HOPE I READ YOUR THOUGHTS…DO I GET THAT MAGAZINE

A SMILE CAN'T ALWAYS BE WITHIN YOUR SPHERE
AND HAPPINESS CAN'T BE CONTROLLED WITHOUT TEARS

YES IT'S LOVE…
BULLY LOVE, PULLEY LOVE
IT WILL WEAR YOU OUT…
MUCH WORK IS NEEDED TO DISPEL DOUBT

WHEN THE TABLE IS FULL…SEAT NO MORE GUESTS
LOVE'S GOLDEN RULE IS TO ALWAYS CREATE MORE TESTS

THE ANSWERS TO YOUR THOUGHTS WON'T ALWAYS BE SEASONED
MYSTERIES WILL ALWAYS PEER AROUND THE CORNER UNREASONED

IT'S LOVE…
BULLY LOVE, WOOLLY LOVE
IT COMES DRESSED IN FEAR
DON'T CLOSE YOUR EYES, IT MAY DISAPPEAR

FALLING DOWN

THOUGHTS OF YOU PASS THROUGH ME
THE SUNLIGHT THROUGH THE TREES PLAYS LIKE A MOVIE

TOO MANY WORDS THAT I CAN'T SPEAK
TOO MANY EMOTIONS INSIDE THAT MAKE ME WEAK

SEVERAL TIMES WE HAVE TRIED TO PAINT IT REAL
SOMETIMES I WONDER IF WE SHOULD HAVE EVER BROKEN LOVE'S SAFETY SEAL

FALLING DOWN, JUST LET ME FALL DOWN
DON'T LET ME FLOAT, LET ME HIT THE GROUND
FALLING DOWN, OUR LOVE IS FALLING DOWN

SOMETIMES YOUR PASSION IS PRISON, A WALLED TOMB
YOUR HEART THE GUARD OF THE VISION…SURVEYS THE ROOM

TEN TIMES THE WEIGHT OF THE WORLD IS THE PRESSURE I KNOW
IS IT A MISTAKE TO JUMP IN TO THE AIR, TO SLIP…TO LET GO

YOU SAY THAT YOU'RE DROWNING IN LOVE'S SOLUTION…
THEN WHY ARE YOUR WORDS SPILLED AND NOT USED THEN

FALLING DOWN, JUST LET ME FALL DOWN
OUR SENTENCE, TOO MANY VERBS AND ONLY ONE NOUN
FALLING DOWN, OUR LOVE IS FALLING DOWN

STATUE POSES, REHEARSED EXPRESSION AND YOUR DIRECTOR'S CHAIR
DEAD ROSES, A BITTER LESSON AND THE FEEL OF HURT'S HARD STARE

CHECKMATE, SEEMS YOU'VE WON AGAIN…BUT WHAT'S THE PRIZE
FLAME-FLICKER, SMOKE AND THEN BLACK…IN THOSE EYES

FROM THE SHADOWS THIS LOVE WAS TAKEN AND TWISTED SEMI-PURE

I'LL MISS THE HIDDEN HOPE OF OUR REALITY, OFF-BALANCE AND NEVER
REALLY SURE

FALLING DOWN, JUST LET ME FALL DOWN
YOU SAY YOU NEED SOME SILENCE, BUT WHAT'S THAT SOUND…
IT'S US FALLING DOWN, OUR LOVE IS FALLING DOWN

A RAINY VALENTINE'S

CONFUSED, YOU'RE CAUGHT BETWEEN SENSIBLE AND SENSITIVE
SOME DAYS YOUR HEART WANTS THE BOX, OTHER DAYS TO LIVE

A COLD FEBRUARY AND YOU WOULDN'T UNFREEZE
THE DRINK IN YOUR BLOOD WOULDN'T WEAKEN YOUR KNEES

A RAINY VALENTINE' S…CUPID'S ARROW HIT THE SUN
CROSS-TALK BETWEEN YOU AND I, SO MUCH FRICTION
CHOCOLATES AND THOUGHTS LAY BESIDE THE BED…
BOTH SEMI-SWEET PLEASURES THAT WE'VE BEEN FED

ALL THAT WE ONCE HAD IS JUST HALF-RHYME
SLOW IS THE GRACE, A SMILING FACE FOR QUIET TIME

WHY DID YOUR WORDS FLOW AGAINST THE TIDE
WHEN DID YOUR LOVE DOCK SHORE-SIDE

A RAINY VALENTINE' S…YOUR TEMPER IS LIKE A VOLUME DIAL
THOUGHTS PARKED IN YOUR HEAD LIKE A CROWDED SHOPPING AISLE
IN THE PIT OF MY STOMACH I FEEL EMPTY AND SICK…
AND THE LINES OF OUR PATHWAY ARE NOW BLURRED THICK

NEW THOUGHTS ARE JUST OLD IDEAS RESURRECTED CLEAN
YOUR HEART RECYCLED THROUGH NO METHOD I'VE EVER SEEN

WHEN YOU TRY TO FORCE LOVE, IT WILL SOON SEVER
MY SHOES HAVE WORN THIN WITH THIS HIGH-NOON ENDEAVOR

A RAINY VALENTINE' S…ON SAND, WE NOW FEEL THE GRIT
LIFE'S CURVES AND ANGLES TWIST…. LOVE JUST WON'T ACQUIT
YOU HOLD ME BY STRINGS, BOTH LONG AND SHORT
YOU'RE THE CRIMINAL, VICTIM AND JUDGE IN THIS PASSION-COURT

LYRICS

(OTHER)

POISE

SHELL-BORN, CHALLENGES HAVE BEEN DEFLECTED
THINLY-WORN, TIME TO TAKE-HOLD AND REDIRECT IT

TAKE A SHOT, IF MISSED, IT'S NOT THE END
AGAIN YOU WILL BREATHE,...EVEN MEND

POISE, POISON NO LONGER HAUNTS THE BLOOD
NOISE, NOW DROWNED IN A SANGUINE FLOOD
IGNITE WHAT WAS OUT OF SIGHT...
ENERGIES ONCE SPILLED ARE COLLECTED AIR TIGHT

YOUR CONFIDENCE HAS BEEN ASLEEP IN THE BACKSEAT
...IT'S TIME TO MAKE THE DREAM FULLY COMPLETE

YOU SHOULD USE YOUR WORRY AND YOUR FLIGHT OF FEET
TO STEADY SHAKY HANDS,...PRESS-OUT THOUGHTS OF DEFEAT

POISE, A ZONE OF SLOW-MOTION MOVEMENT
IT EMPLOYS A STAFF WITH DEVOTION TO IMPROVEMENT
LEARN TO THRIVE IN A FROZEN FRAME
THEN COME ALIVE AND SHAPE YOUR FAME

ONCE YOU MAKE IT HAPPEN, THE FEELING IS NOW KNOWN
IT WILL BE FOREVER INGRAINED TO RETRIEVE AND HONE

GREATNESS, A WEIGHT THAT'S MEASURED ON DIFFERENT SCALES
REMEMBER, GIFTS NEVER CLAIMED ARE LEFT WRAPPED IN RIBBON-TAILS

POISE, CALM SEAS AND SETTLED SAND
IT DESTROYS THE NEGATIVE AND THE UNPLANNED
BOYS FROM MEN ARE SEPARATED HERE…
POISE, TAKE HOLD AND CHOKE THE NECK OF FEAR

SOMETHING LEFT

SOMETIMES YOU NEED A MAP WHEN LIFE STEERS SOUTH
AS BADNESS HAPPENS, A SHARP KNIFE IN YOUR MOUTH

SUCH A THREAT WHEN BOREDOM AND SOLITUDE BECOME YOUR FRIENDS
WHEN THE LUST FOR JOY TURNS A CORNER AND THEN SUDDENLY ENDS

IS THERE SOMETHING LEFT, MAYBE SOME RESIDUE
ANYTHING THAT RESEMBLES THE BETTER YOU
WHAT YOU WERE, SPLENDOR IN A PICTURE FRAME
WHAT YOU'VE BECOME IS FADED BEYOND RECLAIM

YOU CAN FEEL THE ACHE AS THE PROBLEMS BUILD WORTH
AND YOU CAN SEE THE WAKE HELP THE WAVES GIVE BIRTH

THE SKILL TO THINK PAST BLUE-THOUGHTS NOW WANES
AND THE FORCES UNSEEN FIGHT TO CRUMBLE PAST GAINS

IS THERE SOMETHING LEFT, A SPARK BEHIND THE DIM
A HIDDEN SPACE OF SAFETY WHERE HOPE CREEPS IN
DO YOU HAVE A BANK ROLL TO PAY THIS TOLL
JUST HOW THICK IS THE PIECE OF METAL THAT SURROUNDS YOUR SOUL

LIFE, IT'S TV COMMERCIALS AND TRAFFIC…DIFFERENT EVERY DAY
RECEPTION TO IT ALL, WEAK THEN STRONG, BUT ALWAYS GRAY

ROPES THAT USED TO SAVE NOW LAY IN KNOTS WITHOUT USE
CREATIVITY STUCK IN STUPIDITY, A GLUE THAT WON'T LET LOOSE

IS THERE SOMETHING LEFT, SOMETHING REFINED…
GREAT LOCKS AND WALLS OFTEN OBSTRUCT THE DEFINED
YOUR PENNED IDEAS NOW LOST IN THIS HAZE…
ALWAYS PUSHING WHEN ENTERING A NEW PHASE

EVENTS

NOTHING MORE THAN WHAT YOU WOKE-UP WITH TODAY
A BLACK DOG, THAT BLUE FOG AND WALLS TINTED GRAY

YOU SAY THAT SOMEONE BUILT A STOPLIGHT IN YOUR LIVING ROOM
THAT'S RIGHT, NO MOVEMENT IN YOUR HOME…A SEALED TOMB

EVENTS WHICH FORCE YOU TO ACT ARE NOW PRESENT
YOU CAN CHOOSE TO USE HASTE OR BE PATIENT
EVENTS,…NO ONE'S GONNA FIND YOU IN THE BLACK
DON'T WASTE ANY MORE TIME, YOU'D BETTER FIGHT BACK

YOU SAY THAT YOU'VE PLAYED ALL OF THE POKER HANDS
A LOSER, YOU BELIEVE YOUR DREAMS ARE BURIED IN PHARAOHED SANDS

HOPE THAT WAS CHOKED BY A ROPE…AND DESIRE, ASHES BY THE FIRE
TIME…JUST A THIEF IN A BLACK ROBE, PROMISE A SEASONED LIAR

EVENTS, HEY, I'M TALKING TO YOU…
CARING, I'M TRYING TO GET THE ARROW THROUGH
EVENTS, KICK-DOWN THE WORLD AND FOLLOW ME ROUND
WILL YOU RUN TO CATCH THE ESSENCE OF NEW OR STAY UNDERGROUND

NOW, A CUP OF COFFEE AND THAT CIGARETTE ARE YOUR BEST BET
EVEN YOUR STAND-BY VICES DON'T RAISE THE FEELINGS YOU GET

YOUR LIFE IS NOTHING BUT ALPHABET STEW…
AND THERE'S NOT ENOUGH LETTERS TO SPELL HAPPINESS FOR YOU

EVENTS, SOMETIMES THE SCRATCH NEEDS AN ITCH…
NON-SENSE, AN INFECTION, AN AFFECTION OR JUST A RELIEF SWITCH
EVENTS, SOMETIMES A TWISTED SYSTEM WITHOUT HOPE
THEY HAVE TAUGHT US TO SLEEP RATHER THAN TO COPE

LEFTOVER

YOUTHFUL ENERGY TRAPPED IN A LULLABY
I'M SURE I'M NOT THE FIRST TO STAND AT THIS POINT, CHEST-HIGH

SHAVING-CREAM-DREAMS, SOMETIMES THEY CUT AND BLEED
I'M JUST STARING INTO THE MIRROR AGAIN…WONDERING WHAT I NEED

LEFTOVER, FEELINGS I HAD STORED TIGHT
WORDS NOT FISTS STARTED AND ENDED THIS FIGHT
LEFTOVER, AN EMPTY CHEST WITHOUT MY SOUL
A HOLLOW DOME, OUR HOME, BURIED IN A HOLE

I NEED SOME SIZZLE, SOME FLAME TO HEAT MY HEART…
WHAT WAS ONCE COMMONPLACE HAS BEEN INJURED…PULLED APART

SILVER TONES OF A ONCE-COATED-HEART…NOW FADE
LIKE HEADLIGHTS THAT DIP INTO NIGHT, CHANGES MADE

LEFTOVER, THE BRIDGES WE BUILT TOGETHER
WHO KNEW THAT THE SUNSHINE WAS PSEUDO WEATHER
LEFTOVER, DREAMS TINTED BLACK….
MY MIND NOW SHELVES THE WEIGHT OF THIS HURTSTACK

LIFE IS ANTICIPATION, LEARN TO JUMP LEFT OR RIGHT…
SELDOM DOES ONE REMOVE CLOTHING TO REVEAL SKIN THAT'S WHITE

SHADOWS HAVE GREATER SUBSTANCE WHEN THEY MIMIC AND OFFSET
MEMORIES LIKE FINGERTIPS PRESS YOUR NECK, THEN RUB IT TO FORGET

LEFTOVER, CASTLES BUILT…BUT NEVER LIVED IN
SHAME A CURRENT-POOL I KNOW I CAN'T SWIM
LEFTOVER, THE HURT LIKE A DEATH CAN BRING
WHEN RIGHT BOWS TO WRONG, THE ANGELS NEVER SING

BOX-PRESSED

OH GOD, WHAT A WASTE OF MY TALENTS...
WORKING INSIDE A BOX...NINE-TO-FIVE, NO BALANCE

MY EYES ARE TIRED AND MY MIND IS SET TO ROAM
BOREDOM MEANS COUNTING-THE-MINUTES, LET ME GO HOME

I'M BOX-PRESSED, I MUST CONFESS...
LIKE A PREMIUM CIGAR...PACKAGED WITH THE BEST
BOX-PRESSED, THIS SEAL NEEDS TO BE STRIPPED
A TEST, TO FEEL...ONE SHOULD FIRST BE GRIPPED

SUCH A TRAGEDY IS THE REPETITION, THE SAME DAY...EVERY DAY
A REAL LACK OF COMPETITION, SAME ATTITUDE, SAME PAY

JUST ONCE I WOULD LIKE MY SHOT AT THE FIFTEEN
TO BE CENTER-STAGE, SPOTLIGHT HOT, ACTING THE SCENE

I'M BOX-PRESSED, NOW TASTING THE STRESS
NO REAL VIEW OF THE OUTSIDE, FALSE REALITY I GUESS
BOX-PRESSED, LIKE PUSHING A SIZE TEN INTO A SIZE TWO
MUCH LESS, THE FEVER TO PRODUCE A DIFFERENT VIEW

YOU SEE THERE IS NO AD IN THE PAPER FOR SATISFACTION
WHAT THEY FORGET TO TELL YOU IS THAT INDOLENCE IS REALLY AN ACTION

THEY SAY TO BE AT THE TOP WATCH WHAT YOU WEAR...
I SAY GIVE ME DEATH BEFORE I SURRENDER TO THAT DARE

I'M BOX-PRESSED, STILL LOOKING FOR SUCCESS
HOPING THAT DISCOVERY COMES TO MY ADDRESS
COLOR AND NON-COLOR BOTH SHOW A PAIN RANGE
BOX-PRESSED, IN AN INSTANT IT CAN ALL CHANGE

BREATHING SPACE

AN AGGRESSIVE TENDENCY IS COMING TO AN END YOU SEE
WINGS ARE OPEN TO GLIDE, NOT TIGHT TO DIVE SHARPLY

SWING WIDE THE DOORS OF SAFER-THINKING
NOW JUMP BEYOND THE TOPSOIL THAT'S SINKING

BREATHING SPACE, THE DISTANCE BETWEEN THE LINES IN YOUR FACE
(MORE) BREATHING SPACE, TAKE IN THE AIR OUTSIDE THE CASE
...GET SOME BREATHING SPACE

PRESSURE TO BUILD GREAT WORKS...EVER PRESENT
THE GOAL, A LIBRARY OR STATUE CAST IN CEMENT

GREATNESS IS ONLY PRESERVED BY GENERATIONS POST
CAN WE DETERMINE NEED OVER WANT, MANY VERSUS MOST

BREATHING SPACE, THE REST THAT LIES BENEATH A HURRIED PACE
(MORE) BREATHING SPACE, WHERE THE WORK AND THE WORRY DISPLACE
...WE ALL NEED SOME BREATHING SPACE

THE BALANCE OF WEIGHT WILL ALWAYS SHIFT
OUR ARMS GETTING USE TO THE PAIN EVERY LIFT

RENTAL CARS DRIVE MANY SPIRITS TODAY
HIGH MILEAGE AND GRAY FABRIC UNDERNEATH THE PEEL-AWAY

BREATHING SPACE, WHITE WAITING ROOM WITH A FLOWERED VASE
(NEEDED) BREATHING SPACE, A TIME TO LEAD RATHER THAN CHASE
INHALE THEN EXHALE...BREATHING SPACE

COMFORT ZONE

I NEVER STUDIED TO BE A STAND-IN…
I ALWAYS THOUGHT MY COURSE WOULD NET A PLANNED WIN

PROBLEMS…YOU'VE GOT A COOLER RELIGION TO BLAME…
BUT TODAY OUR INTRIGUE IS SEEMINGLY QUITE THE SAME

WHAT HAPPENED TO YOUR COMFORT ZONE
YOU USED TO WANT FOR NOT, NEVER ALONE
SUCH A TEMPER YOU NOW LET LIVE
YOUR COMFORT ZONE,…SO SENSITIVE

TIME RUNS SLOW NEXT TO YOU…TICK TOCK
TIRE TRACKS THAT'S WHAT I'M USED TOO, NOT A ROADBLOCK

SEASONS USED TO BE SESSIONS WERE I WOULD TRY TO COPE
DEMONS, NOW BLESSINGS, SWING FREELY WITH NEW ROPE

WHAT HAPPENED TO YOUR COMFORT ZONE
WHAT HAPPENED TO THE LIGHT THAT WAS ONCE SHOWN
I GUESS YOU NEEDED TO STEP OUTSIDE THE BOX
YOUR COMFORT ZONE…BOUND BY COMBINATION LOCKS

I'D LIKE TO TAKE A SLEDGE-HAMMER TO YOUR IMAGINATION
BREAK IT ALL AWAY, SHATTER THE EGO OF FALSIFICATION

SOMETIMES I FAKE IT, BUT NEVER WITH YOU
YET THE LOVE RETURNED FEELS LIKE SUPER GLUE

WHAT HAPPENED TO YOUR COMFORT ZONE
IT SEEMS LIKE ITS BEEN STRETCHED OR EVEN BLOWN
WHAT WILL IT TAKE TO RETURN TO THE ROUTINE
YOUR COMFORT ZONE, A BLANKET-TRAP…UNSEEN

INTO THE MIX

LONG LINES THAT CHANGE WHEN ON THE MOVE
SHORT FEELINGS WHEN I THINK SHE HAS SOMETHING TO PROVE

HER BLANKET…ALWAYS CLOUD-COVER…WITH MY RAINFALL LOVER
THIS PASSION-PLAY I'LL SAVE FOR ANOTHER DAY…JUST THINKING OF HER

INTO THE MIX AS THEY SAY…. SPIN IT AROUND
ALL THE TIMES I USED TO PRAY…MY WINGS NEVER LEFT THE GROUND
I PRESS MY CARDS BUT NEVER FOLD…
TO BLUFF WOULD BE ROUGH AND I'M GETTING TOO OLD

HER DESIGN…. ENGINEERED BY GOD AND POWERED BY FATE
SHE'S SOMETHING OF A MYSTERY…NOTHING I ANTICIPATE

DECISION IS NOT HER SISTER, FRIEND OR JURY
HER PROBLEMS STAND IN CONCRETE, THE ANSWERS COME IN NO HURRY

INTO THE MIX AS THEY SAY…. SPIN IT AROUND
MY BODY FLOATS TO THE SURFACE, MY HEAD DROWNED
I PRESS MY CARDS BUT NEVER FOLD…
TO GAIN WEALTH YOU MUST SPEND SOME GOLD

SHE'S THE WEAPON AND THE INJURY, READ HER BOOK
OH HOW SHE LOVES TO PLAY WITH ME…THAT SUBTLE LOOK

SHE'LL PUT ME ON THE BACK BURNER AND THEN INTO THE OVEN
ALWAYS ICE CUBES AND FIRE WHEN SHE'S PUSHIN' AND SHOVIN'

INTO THE MIX AS THEY SAY…. SPIN IT AROUND
BREAKING AWAY FROM THIS PACK OF HOUNDS
I PRESS MY CARDS BUT NEVER FOLD…
PAYING MY DEBT FROM THE SINS I'VE SOLD

ANY-DAY-GIRL (FUN SONG-SPOOF)

SHE GETS SO MAD AT ME…WHEN I WATCH TV
SHE WOULD HIT ME [JUST TO SIT ME} NEXT TO COURTESY

DOESN'T SHE KNOW THAT SHE'S MY MONDAY SHOW
DOESN'T SHE SEE…SHE MEANS NOTHING TO ME

SHE'S MY ANY-DAY-GIRL…
SHE'S THE NUT AND I'M THE SQUIRREL
WHEN WILL SHE UNDERSTAND THE SIMPLE DEAL
SHE'S JUST MY ANY-DAY-GIRL-HAPPY-MEAL

SHE REALLY HATES ME WHEN…I GET DRUNK AGAIN
SHE WANTS TO TURN ME IN, KEEP ME IN A PEN

DOESN'T SHE CARE SHE'S TUESDAY'S UNDERWEAR
DOESN'T SHE WISH FOR A BETTER CATCH OF FISH

SHE'S MY ANY-DAY-GIRL…
I'M A SINGLE MAN, NO NEED TO BE PLURAL
WHEN WILL SHE UNDERSTAND MY LIFE
SHE'S JUST AN ANY-DAY-GIRL…NOT MY WIFE

SHE LIKES ME TO BE SO NICE AND NEAT, REALLY SWEET…
SHE WANTS MY CLOTHES TO MATCH, NOT TO SCRATCH AND LOTS OF HEAT

DOESN'T SHE GRIP THAT SHE'S MY WEDNESDAY TRIP
A VACATION SPOT WHERE THE PIGEONS SQUAT

SHE'S MY ANY-DAY-GIRL…
THE MOON AROUND MY EARTHLY WORLD
JUST A SATELLITE ON A THURSDAY NIGHT
SHE'S JUST AN ANY-DAY-GIRL, MY GIRL…. THAT'S RIGHT

ANY-DAY GIRL
ANY-DAY-GIRL
ANY-DAY-GIRL…

SUGARCANE

SITUATIONS OF TROUBLE HAVE A ROPE AROUND YOUR HEART
YOUR GLASS-CASING IS SPLINTERED, MELTING…BREAKING APART

TODAY YOU COUNTED FAILURES, ONE LABELED "GOOD" THIRTEEN STAMPED "HURT "
YOU WONDER…CAN ONE SWIM THROUGH MUD WITHOUT TASTING THE DIRT

OPENING PASSION IS LIKE UNSEALING BOTTLED WINE
YOU NEVER KNOW IF THE AIR WILL BE CRUEL OR KIND

SUGARCANE…
LET ME EASE YOUR PAIN
TAKE IT EASY…
YOU DON'T ALWAYS HAVE TO PLEASE ME

I HAVE MANY THEORIES TO BRING YOUR COLOR BACK
I WILL BECOME YOUR ARMY, PURSUE THE ENEMY…LET YOU REST FROM THE ATTACK

I KNOW YOU'RE INDEPENDENT, YOU OFTEN WANT TO SWING THE SWORD
BUT YOU CAN'T CONTINUE UNLESS YOU DRINK THE WATER THAT WAS PREVIOUSLY POURED

TIE-UP ALL THOSE FEELINGS WITH A EMOTIONAL TOURNIQUET
AND PUSH AWAY YOUR CHAIR FROM THE FESTIVAL BANQUET

SUGARCANE…
LET ME LIGHTEN THE STAIN
SKIN, IT'S SUCH A SUPERFICIAL SUNDAE
SIN, DON'T YOU KNOW IT ALWAYS BEGINS ON MONDAY

A HEART…DOES IT ALWAYS NEED TO BE TOUCHED BY A HELPING HAND
I'VE SEEN THE LOVE FILL-UP IN YOUR EYES AND WONDER WHAT'S BEING PLANNED

IS IT THE STARS THAT CALL TO YOUR SOUL…COME FLY SKYWARD
CAN I CUT THE CHAINS THAT TIE, BECOME YOUR WINGS…FREE YOUR BIRDS

LIKE A CEMENT WALL, YEARS LEAVE YOU CRACKED AND NOW BLEACHED
LET ME MASON YOUR SHELL AND BIND THE FABRIC THAT HAS BEEN TORN AND
SO OFTEN BREACHED

SUGARCANE…
LIKE SULLEN RAIN…
ONTO SKIN, YOU COME THEN PASS
I'M JUST A FLY BENEATH YOUR GLASS
I'M KNOCKING AT YOUR WHITE DOOR
BREATH UNTO BREATH, I WANT MORE

TIME

A CAMERA FLASHES…YOUR LIFE IS OVER
YOU PLAYED YOUR HAND…NOW YOU'RE THE JOKER

YOU ALWAYS EXPECTED A MUCH SLOWER PACE
YET THOSE LINES WERE ADDED SO QUICKLY TO YOUR FACE

WHAT TO DO WITH THE MEMORIES OF YOUTH
DO YOU TELL OTHERS YOUR SECRETS, YOUR LIES, YOUR TRUTH

TIME, THAT THIEF WE ALL ROB WITH
TIME, TO STOP ITS TACTICS WOULD BE A DELUSIONAL MYTH
YOU'LL NEVER TRAP IT AND YOU'LL NEVER SEE IT CHEW
BUT BELIEVE ME MY FRIEND IT WILL CAPTURE YOU

OH, TO TRADE A DAY IN YOUR LIFE FOR ANOTHER
A KISS FROM YOUR WIFE ON THE FIRST DATE, THE LAST HUG YOU EVER
RECEIVED FROM YOUR MOTHER

YOUR HANDS, FORMERLY STRONG…WITH HANDSHAKES SO BOLD
YOUR EYES, WITHOUT GLASSES…WAITING TO BEHOLD

WHAT HAPPENED TO YESTERDAY…
YOU THOUGHT THIS MOVIE WAS MORE THAN JUST A MATINEE´
TIME, THE SPACE BETWEEN HERE AND THERE
TIME, THE CHANGING COLOR OF YOUR HAIR
A BALANCED-BEAM WE ALL WALK AND WE ALL FALL
A LION AND LAMB, IT WILL SOMETIMES LEAP THEN SLOW TO A CRAWL

PLEASE BRING HIM HIS WINE
A FEW SIPS AND EVERYTHING WILL BE FINE

TO REST IN PEACE MEANS TO BE LEFT ALONE
PEOPLE WANT COMPANY FOREVER…THEIR TELEVISION, THEIR PHONE

JUST REMEMBER, AS OPEN CONTAINERS OFTEN GET FILLED
…PITCHERS TO FULL WILL SURELY GET SPILLED

TIME, BLENDED, WELL-AGED SCOTCH
TIME, THIS BAR WILL ALWAYS SERVE MIXED SHOTS
NEVER CONSCIOUS OF YOUR CONSCIENCE, IT DOESN'T DISCRIMINATE
IT WILL FOREVER BE YOUR JUDGE AND JURY POISED TO INCRIMINATE

HIGHER

WHO CAN TELL YOU HOW HIGH YOUR STAR SHOULD DRAPE
DON'T FEAR THE HEIGHTS YOU CLIMB, IT'S OKAY TO ESCAPE

ALWAYS MAINTAIN THE VISION TO SEE, NEVER LOOSE THE KEYS THAT FREE
BE RICH BUT ALWAYS MAINTAIN YOUR ANONYMITY

EVER ASK YOURSELF WHO PUSHES YOUR ACCELERATOR
EVER WONDER HOW MANY MILES LEFT ON YOUR ODOMETER

HIGHER, NOT AN ELEVATION BUT AN AWAKENED STATE
HIGHER, A REVELATION HOW TO BE GREAT
BUILDING ON THE FOUNDATION DETECTED BELOW…
YOU ENCOUNTER AN EAGLE'S VIEW BUT CONTINUE TO FLY LOW

WILL YOU HANDS BE UNSTAINED WHEN YOUR JOURNEY'S DONE
OR WILL YOU FIND THAT YOU HANDS HAVE BEEN DIRTIED BY HURTING SOME-
ONE

AS THE CENTER LINE BECOMES YOUR GUIDE ON THIS HIGHWAY
WILL YOU STAY STRAIGHT, CROSS-OVER OR ACCIDENTALLY SWAY

NO ONE CAN AVOID THEIR OWN CONTINUING COUNT-DOWN
WHAT DID YOU SEE AFTER LIFT-OFF WHEN YOU LOOKED AT THE GROUND

HIGHER, A PLACE THAT REACHES BEYOND YOUR LINES
HIGHER, A CHECK THAT YOUR HEART CASHES BUT YOUR MIND SIGNS
MAKE A PROMISE TO BECOME WHAT'S REAL
OPEN ENVELOPE S UNKNOWN, SHARE FORTUNES WITH THOSE THAT STEAL

TO BE FAMOUS YOU HAVE TO BE EMBRACED
TO FEED YOU MUST EAT ALWAYS SMELLING TO TASTE

REMEMBER, THE SUN AND MOON BOTH RISE AND FALL
HAPPINESS IS BOTH SUNSHINE AND DARKNESS...HEED THE CALL

HEARTACHE...IT CAN BE TOLD BY THE FOLDING OF CLOTHES
IS YOUR HEART WRINKLED OR PLEATED, WE ALL SEEM TO SMELL A DIFFERENT
ROSE

HIGHER, WHEN THE ALTITUDE BECOMES AIR-THIN
HIGHER, WHEN YOU OVERCOME OR SURRENDER...YET YOU STILL WIN
SHARPEN YOUR SPIKES AND BEGIN TO CLIMB
HIGHER...DON'T YOU THINK IT'S TIME...

OPENINGS

FEELINGS RISE LIKE GHOSTS FROM MY SKIN, IT'S A COMBINATION MONDAY
I'M HOT AND COLD, OUT THEN IN, TODAY SHOULD BE A DONE-DAY

I WALK THROUGH WAVES OF GLASS AND I'M CUT AS THEY SCRAPE PAST
I KNOW I'M ON WINDOW-DISPLAY, MARTINI-MIXED IN THIS NARROWED FLASK

TRAIN STATIONS ARE WAIT STATIONS, YOUR LIFE A STEEL TRACK
THE RAIL CARS ARE THE FREIGHT THAT YOU FEEL STRAPPED TO YOUR BACK

THE OPENING OF CERTAIN CANS...
WILL DRAIN YOUR HEART OF ALL PLANS
YOU'LL FEEL AS IF YOU'RE SWIMMING, THEN SPINNING WHEN THE TIME COMES
YOU'LL SURELY LOSE YOUR EQUILIBRIUM

THERE IS NO ONE OF THE FLESH THAT DOESN'T FEEL THE STING
EVERYONE FEELS PAIN WHEN LETTING GO OF SOMETHING

WILL YOU BUILD YOUR SKYSCRAPERS
OR WILL YOU CLEAN THE OLDER MONUMENTS WITH SANDPAPER

HOTEL HAVENS WERE NEVER REALLY YOUR STYLE
CIRCLED BY HUNGRY RAVENS, YOU STEP FROM THIS WAIST-HIGH GARBAGE PILE

THE OPENING OF CERTAIN CANS...
WILL BREAK THE SEAL OF ANY MAN
YOU'LL FEEL AS IF YOU'RE LEASING YOUR OWN SOUL
AS YOU'RE THROWN INTO THE DEVIL'S DARKENED HOLE

THEY ALWAYS BITE BELOW THE COLLAR SO NO ONE SEES THE MARK
WITH TUNNEL VISION IT'S TOUGH TO PLAY YOUR CARDS IN THE DARK

HOW MANY TEARS ADD-UP TO EQUAL A MINUTE OF TIME
HOW MANY JUMPS FROM A PLANE DOES IT TAKE TO KNOW HOW HIGH YOU'VE
CLIMBED

SUBMERGED BY LOUD WORDS, I FIND MY SELF WITHOUT AIR
LACK OF OXYGEN WHEN CONVERSATION COMES TENDS TO ALWAYS SCARE

THE OPENING OF CERTAIN CANS...
WILL TURN YOUR WORKS OF WONDER INTO THE COLORINGS OF CRAYON
ARE YOU STAINED FROM THE CONTENTS WHICH WERE NEVER POURED
OR ARE YOU FAMOUS FROM RECEIVING THE JUDAS' REWARD

PAYMENTS

SPEAK EASY WHEN THINGS DON'T DISSOLVE
WITH FAITH THERE'S NOTHING A KIND KISS WON'T SOLVE

WAIVE TO YOUR ENEMIES WHEN THEY STONE-STARE
QUICK-SHOVEL DIRT FROM THE PILES OF FEELINGS IN YOUR CARE

SET A TABLE THAT EXCLUDES SHARP KNIVES
STEP-CLIMB OVER WALLS INTO OTHER LIVES

PAYMENTS…EVERYONE OWES IN LIFE
PAYMENTS…DEBT TO OTHERS, YOUR FIRST WIFE
GIVE TO ALL WHO ARE IN NEED
CAST OUT YOUR SPIRIT'S APPETITE FOR GREED

BOTTLE THE SCENTS OF PASSION AND PEACE
SPRAY-PAINT THE LIES THAT DISCOLOR YOUR TEETH

CUT THE HAIR THAT KINKS YOUR VISION
SHOWER-SOFTEN ANGER WITH PATIENCE AND PRECISION

DEFROST YOUR SOUL WHEN IT'S COVERED IN ICE
MICROWAVE YOUR LOVE ON HIGH-SETTING, TWICE

PAYMENTS…SIGN THE CHECK
PAYMENTS…BOTH LOW AND HIGH-TECH
REMEMBER TO ALWAYS WEAVE A COAT OF TRUST
SITUATIONS WILL SURELY DICTATE WHEN YOU OFTEN CAN'T OR TRULY MUST

GATHER YOUR WATER FROM THE DEEPEST OF WELLS
BARTER FOR THE BLOOD YOUR HEART NO LONGER EXPELS

MOLD YOUR BODY FROM CLAY TO POTTERY
BELIEVE HOPE IS THE WINDFALL IN YOUR STATE-OF-MIND LOTTERY

BLUE-SKY

I WANT BLUE SKY
A PIECE OF THE EVER ELUDING APPLE PIE

TO DIVE TO THE BOTTOMS OF DEEP WELLS
TO MINISTER MY THOUGHTS FROM THE TOWERS OF BELLS

SMOKE FLOATS INTO EYES THAT ARE OPEN…BUT NEVER BLINK
IMPATIENCE AND HURRIED ACTIONS OFTEN RISE BUT ALWAYS SINK

I WANT BLUE SKY…
LUXURIES TO OWN…. NOT RENT-TO-BUY
NO DARKENED DESIGNS PASTED ON MY BULLETIN-BOARD
GRAVITY NEEDS TO PULL ME CLOSER TO THE OBJECTS I'M RUNNING TOWARD

LISTEN TO THE TREES AS THEIR LEAVES SPEAK THROUGH THE WIND
THE EARTH SPEAKS TO ALL, REMINDING EACH THAT THEY HAVE SINNED

THE GRASS-CARPET BEGS YOU TO REST YOUR HEAD
THE WATERWAYS REMIND YOU OF EMOTIONS THAT CAN'T BE PRE-READ

I WANT TO UNCOVER THE EARTH AND BATH IN ITS SOIL
TO BE KING OF MY HILL BUT STILL SERVE THE HEAVENS SUBJECTIVE AND LOYAL

I WANT BLUE SKY…
TO BE BOLD AND COMMANDING…YET SHY
TO SWIRL COLOR INTO THIS GREAT GRAY MIX
BECOMING A PHYSICIAN TO MY BODY AS I STERILIZE THEN STITCH

I WILL SOMEDAY TAKE MANY GREAT BREATHS OF AIR
EMERGE TO TAKE-HOLD AND CHOKE THE THROAT OF DESPAIR

IN THE QUIET HOURS I CONTINUE TO PRESENT MY PRESENCE TASTEFULLY
WHEN CHANCE CALLS I WILL CERTAINLY ANSWER THE PHONE HASTEFULLY

I WANT BLUE SKY
TO BE AT PEACE AND TO KNOW I GOT A PIECE WHEN I DIE
TO TRAVEL DOWN DIMLY-LIT ROADS AT TWILIGHT
KNOWING THAT WITH EACH NEW SUN COMES CLOUDLESS SUNLIGHT

EXTRA

LIFE, IT SWELLS LIKE A WAVE THEN RETREATS FROM THE SAND
WE ALL TEETER ON THE EDGE WHEN OUR FUTURE IS UNPLANNED

I DON'T WANT TO WEAR THIS DIRTY SHIRT ANYMORE
IT SEEMS THE SINS ON MY SLEEVE DON'T COME CLEAN ON SPIN-CYCLE FOUR

THE SHORE ACROSS THE RIVER CALLS TO ME
I SEEM TO LIKE THE ELEMENT OF INCONSISTENCY

AIR AND TIME THAT'S WHAT I NEED
AIR AND TIME TO PLANT THE SEED
I'M TURNING BLUE AS I BREATHE THROUGH THIS HOSE
I FEEL LIKE A TREE THAT HAS BEEN BLED BY AX-HANDLED FOES

I WANT TO PLAY CHESS WITH THE VOICES IN MY HEAD
TO FLIP-OVER THE COMMONWEALTH MATTRESS WHICH FORMS MY BED

I'LL RACE AROUND THE TRACK
NOT TO LAP OTHERS, JUST TO BREAK-FREE FROM THE PACK

OH, TO PURSUE THAT WHICH ELUDES
TO POUND EACH POINT WHICH PROTRUDES

AIR AND TIME THAT'S WHAT I NEED
AIR AND TIME TO TAKE THE LEAD
A SIMPLE MAN WITH A COMPLEX DECISION
WILL I EVER FIND THE IDEA THAT FRAMES MY VISION

ONE'S SPIRIT MUST ALWAYS BE FED
AS TIME SEEMS TO SWALLOW THE TRUTH AND REGURGITATE THE ALLEGED

HOW OFTEN DOES A MAN STAND WHEN HIS FELLOW MEN SIT
HOW OFTEN DOES ONE TAKE A CHISEL TO STONE AND SCULPT IT

LET ME PULL-UP ANCHOR AND DRIFT OUT TO SEA
LET ME DROWN IN THIS SENSATION CALLED OPPORTUNITY

AIR AND TIME THAT 'S WHAT I NEED
AIR AND TIME TO FINALLY SUCCEED
GOD PLEASE ALLOW ME TO LIFT THE NEXT STONE
AND LET ME LIVE TO OVERCOME THE WORD ALONE

GET-AWAY

UNSETTLING MUSIC…UNSETTLED SOUL
DAD'S GOING THROUGH MID-LIFE, MOTHER'S IN THE HOLE

DAMN THOSE GRAY SKIES, THOSE RAIN DROPS SEEP IN
LOTS OF DARKENED LIES, IT'S BETTER IF WE JUST SLEEP IN

THE GROUND IS SOAKED BY GRIEF AND MY FEET SINK DEEP
THERE'S NO LADDER OR ROPE TO PREVENT THIS CANYON LEAP

SOMETIMES IT SEEMS…TO WORRY IS DEATH
THESE FEELINGS CAN INCREASE WITH EVERY BREATH
TRAFFIC-LIGHTS FLICKER AND WE ALL OBEY
DON'T YOU WISH YOU COULD JUST GET AWAY

ARE WE ALL JUST CANDLES ON A BIG BIRTHDAY CAKE
STARS IN THE SKY…RIPPLES ON A LAKE

THE COLD WEATHER PUSHES MY EMOTIONS FIRMLY IN
TWO SHOTS DOWN AND I NO LONGER FEEL MY OUTER SKIN

DO YOU WANT TO STRAY FROM YOUR DREAM'S LANDSCAPE
WILL YOU TIGHTEN YOUR GRIP OR STRETCH THE FABRIC SO THE SEAMS DRAPE

DOLLAR BILLS WON'T EVER TALK BACK TO YOU
AND YOUR SPORTS CAR CAN'T CHANGE Its DASHBOARD VIEW
SHOULDN'T THE SIMPLE THINGS BREAK THOROUGH…SOMEDAY
DON'T YOU WISH YOU COULD JUST GET AWAY

WHAT DEEPENED GROOVE DOESN'T FLATTEN TIRES ON A HIGHWAY
WHAT LIES EVER SHIELD YOUR HEART'S CORE ALL OF THE WAY

HAPPINESS…A PAPER-THIN BAG, A PUPPET WHEN TURNED ABOUT
WHO HASN'T HAD AN ILLNESS AND LOOKED FOR THE OBVIOUS WAY-OUT

OH…ARE THE RULES OUR MAPPED-GUIDE OR PRISON FENCE
JUST WHAT IS THE MAKE-UP OF OUR SELF-CONFIDENCE

HANGING ONTO FEELINGS TOO TIGHTLY
WE SHOULD ACT ON INSTINCT AND STOP ACTING POLITELY
REPLACE THE FABRIC THAT HAS FADED AND HAS BEGUN TO FRAY
…. DROP IT ALL AND JUST GET AWAY

28

HEAVY WEIGHTS AND PRISON BREAKS...
ALL WITHIN THE CONFINES OF MY ALTERED STATES

HERE THE PAINT NEVER COVERS THE WALLS
SHADOWS BLOCK THE RAYS WHERE THE SUNLIGHT FALLS

THE STAIRS WILL ALWAYS LEAD TO THE TOP
BUT THERE ARE NO RAILINGS TO PREVENT YOUR EVENTUAL DROP

TWENTY-EIGHT, SOMETIMES IN A SLEEP-STATE
MY EYES GROW COLDER AS I CLOSE MY FRONT GATE
THE BARS BEND BUT NEVER SEEM TO BREAK
THE FLOOR-BOARDS CONTINUE TO BEAR MY LATEST ACHES

EACH TOWER HERE HOLDS A DIFFERENT FELON
THE THIEVES, MURDERERS AND EMBEZZLERS ARE ALL SELLIN'

THERE ARE TIMES WHEN I NEED TO SQUEEZE-OUT ALL THAT I AM
BUT THERE ARE TIMES WHEN I JUST DON'T GIVE A DAMN

I MUST PRESS THROUGH, RACE HARD AND KICK WIDE
I NEED TO SEPARATE THE OUT FROM THE INSIDE

TWENTY-EIGHT, SOMETIMES IN A SLEEP-STATE
FREEDOM, SOMETIMES SEEMS LIKE A JOURNEY I CAN'T MAKE
OH, WHAT IS THE LENGTH I HAVE TO WAIT
CAN'T I EVER DANCE WITHOUT FATE

IN HERE MY PROMISES ARE KEPT IN A CRAWL-SPACE
POLICE TAPE SURROUNDS THE OPENINGS AT EVERY FACE

SOLITARY CONFINEMENT IS THE CURSE OF THIS CELL
ALONE WITH MY THOUGHTS AND NO ONE TO TELL

TO EVER BREAK-OUT WOULD MEAN THAT I COULD DIE
BUT TO CHANGE WE MUST LEARN AND TO LEARN WE MUST TRY

TWENTY-EIGHT, SOMETIMES IN A SLEEP-STATE
I OFTEN FEEL LIKE FISH-BAIT
WHY DON'T THEY JUST STUFF ME OR PUT ME ON A PLATE
IF THERE'S LEFT-OVERS…PLEASE REFRIGERATE

TWENTY-EIGHT, SOMETIMES IN A SLEEP-STATE…

TOUCH

YOU BUILD YOUR FIRE TO BURN SOMETHING NEW
A TWENTY-FOUR-HOUR-HEADACHE, NO PILL CURES YOU

LET ME GIVE BACK WHAT OTHERS HAVE DESTROYED
INSIDE YOU HEART I'LL PLAY CUPID, INSIDE YOUR HEAD…FREUD

I'LL BE THE NEW SKIN WHEN YOU SHED THE OLD
I'LL BE THE FIRE WHEN YOUR THOUGHTS TURN COLD

TALK VERSUS TOUCH VERSUS FEEL
GIVE FREELY OR STEAL
TALK VERSUS TOUCH VERSUS FEEL
TAKE THE TIME TO HEAL

I'LL BUILD YOU A BRIDGE WHEN I TEAR-DOWN YOUR WALLS
BE THE BUSY SIGNAL WHEN THIS EVER-WANTING WORLD CALLS

LET ME LIFT THE WEIGHT YOU WEAR ON YOUR FACE
TRANSPORT YOUR PAIN TO ANOTHER PLACE

I'LL PULL THE WEEDS THAT ENTANGLE YOU
PLANT THE SEEDS WHERE NOTHING EVER GREW…IN YOUR HEART

TALK VERSUS TOUCH VERSUS FEEL
EVENTUALLY EVERYONE NEEDS TO KNEEL
TALK VERSUS TOUCH VERSUS FEEL
COME, LET'S MAKE A DEAL

I WON'T EVER BE THE FENCE THAT SURROUNDS
I'LL BE THE SILENCE DRIVING AWAY THE SOUNDS

JUST WANT TO MAKE YOU BELIEVE…
I CAN OFFER GIFTS YOU CAN ONLY RECEIVE

LOVE...IT'S JUST AROUND THE CORNER
ITS WORLD WAITS FOR YOU TO BE BORN THERE

TALK VERSUS TOUCH VERSUS FEEL
IT'S YOUR TURN TO SPIN THE WHEEL
TALK VERSUS TOUCH VERSUS FEEL
CAN WE MAKE IT REAL...

TONIGHT

TONIGHT I STOPPED AND LISTENED TO THE EARTH
TRIED TO FIGURE-OUT WHO I WAS, WHAT I'M WORTH

CLOUDS IN THE SKY, CITY LIGHTS, A LOT FULL OF CARS
AN OBSERVER, A SERVER, ONE WHO WANTS THE STARS

WILL I EVER MAKE THE SWITCH, EVER PULL THE SWITCH
WAITING, THIN-ICE SKATING, SCRATCHIN' THE ITCH

TONIGHT I SEARCH TO FIND ANOTHER STATE OF MIND
I'LL SUCCEED MY FORMER UNION, BREAK ALL BINDS
TONIGHT I LOSE THE OLD ME
JUST WAIT AND SEE…

I'VE BEEN UNEVEN FOR YEARS, MY ROAD INCLINED
PLANTED, ROOTED, ONLY RECEIVING FILTERED SUNSHINE

OH THE STEPS WE CLIMB, BETTER HOLD THE RAILING
NEVER SURE-FOOTED ALL OF THE TIME, ALWAYS SCALING

TONIGHT ALL WILL FINALLY CHANGE
YOU'LL AGAIN SEE MY LION'S MANGE
TONIGHT MY STORY WILL REWRITE ITS ENDING
THE WORLD WILL FINALLY RECEIVE THE MESSAGE I'M SENDING

UNGRATEFUL SOMETIMES, FEELING SOMETHING'S MISSING
I HAVE TO BE COME REBORN, STOP THIS REMINISCING

JUST WANT TO FEEL MY SOUL, TO KNOW I CAN REACH MY GOAL
TO FEAST ON SUCCESS UNINVITED AND EMPTY THE BOWL

NO MORE BREAKING DOWN, ONLY BREAKING-OUT
THE MAN OF YESTERDAY HAS BEEN SEIZED AND CAST ABOUT

TONIGHT I'LL STOP THE ROTATION BETWEEN NOW AND THEN
TONIGHT I'LL GET COMFORTABLE IN MY OWN SKIN
TONIGHT I'LL RAISE THE ROOF TWICE ITS HEIGHT
TONIGHT I WILL WIN THIS FIGHT

EVER

EVER LISTENED TO THE VOICES IN YOUR HEAD
EVER STARVE THE DEMONS YOU JUST FED

EVER REACH FOR THE SKY AND HIT THE CEILING
EVER PRAY TO GOD TO STOP WHAT YOU'RE FEELING

EVER…
YOUR HOPES AND FEARS
THOSE MANY YEARS
YOUR NOW AND NEVER

EVER COVER YOUR HEART IN HOPES TO SEAL
EVER USE A STRANGER TO HELP YOU HEAL

EVER WAKE-UP ROUGH THEN DRINK TO BE SMOOTH
EVER FLOAT LIKE DUST BUT NEVER MOVE

EVER HAVE YOUR APPETITE GO ON A DIET
EVER CONDEMN SOMETHING BEFORE YOU TRY IT

EVER…
CHANCES YOU WANT TO TAKE
DECISIONS YOU HAD TO MAKE
GO AHEAD PULL THE LEVER

EVER THROW WORDS TO SOMEONE WHO COULDN'T CATCH
EVER BURNED A LOVER WITHOUT A MATCH

EVER GRASP FURTHER THAN YOU COULD REACH
EVER LOSE YOUR PULPIT WHEN YOU WANTED TO PREACH

EVER FEEL LIKE A LONE CAR IN A PARKING LOT
EVER SET YOUR SIGHTS BUT NEVER TAKE THE SHOT

EVER…
WHAT YOU CAN AND CAN'T SEE
WHO YOU ARE AND WANT TO BE
SOME WANTS YOU NEED TO SEVER

WILL YOU CHANGE YOUR PREDICTED NEVER…EVER

BROWN WRAPPER

FOREIGN ROOM, CONVERSATION IS LIGHT
SITUATIONS LOOM, THE AIR IS HEAVY TONIGHT

STAR-STRUCK ARE THE LOCAL FACES
TURN-UP THE VOLUME, ADJUST YOUR SOCIAL GRACES

"BRUBECK" IN THE BACKGROUND AS SPACE IS TIGHT
STORIES ARE THICK AND REHEARSED, DID YOU BRING YOUR INVITE

BROWN WRAPPER IS WHAT THEY CALL THIS PLACE
HERE, THEY WILL BLOW SMOKE IN YOUR FACE
IT WILL BE MY PLEASURE TO GET YOU IN…
OH…LET THE GOOD TIMES BEGIN

MR. FUENTE, HE'S MY FRIEND
HE NEEDS A MATCH EVERY NOW AND THEN

IF YOU NEED A DRINK…IT NEEDS YOU TOO
HERE THERE'S PLENTY OF LIQUID TO BATHE YOU NEW

THE SCENT OF CEDAR, WARM WALNUT THE DECOR
ME AND HER, THE THOUGHT AS SHE ENTERS THE DOOR

SPECIAL TIMES THAT'S WHAT THEY SELL
THERE'S THE MATRON, SHE'S CASTING HER DREAM-SPELL
A NEW WATCH AND CLOTHES TO LOOK DAPPER
EVERYTHING IS POSSIBLE AT THE BROWN WRAPPER

YOU DON'T NEED CASH OR CREDIT CARD WHEN IN NEED…
THE WRAPPER JUST WANTS YOUR SOUL, PLEASE SIGN THE DEED

CONFESSING SINS AND REPENTING WORDS WON'T BREAK YOUR TIE
THE EXIT DOOR FOREVER SPINS ROUND, LEAVING IS BEGINNING…WHEN LIVING A LIE

BROWN WRAPPER, YOU WRAP ME UP
BROWN WRAPPER……………………..HIC-UP!

BROWN WRAPPER IS WHAT THEY CALL THIS PLACE
HERE, THEY WILL BLOW SMOKE IN YOUR FACE
IT WILL BE MY PLEASURE TO GET YOU IN…
OH…LET THE GOOD TIMES BEGIN

PAYMENT OF LOVE (1)

LONG LINES THAT CHANGE WHEN ON THE MOVE
SHORT FEELINGS WHEN I THINK SHE HAS SOMETHING TO PROVE

HER BLANKET…ALWAYS CLOUD-COVER…WITH MY RAINFALL LOVER
THIS PASSION-PLAY I'LL SAVE FOR ANOTHER DAY…JUST THINKING OF HER

A MISSED PAYMENT OF LOVE
A DELAYED PUSH…THEN SHOVE
MY SIGHT…NOTHING BUT BLURRED VISION
ON THE EAST SIDE OF HER WITHOUT THE SUN

I PRESS MY CARDS BUT NEVER FOLD…
TO BLUFF WOULD BE ROUGH AND I'M GETTING TOO OLD

HER DESIGN…. ENGINEERED BY GOD AND POWERED BY FATE
SHE'S SOMETHING OF A MYSTERY…NOTHING I ANTICIPATE

A MISSED PAYMENT OF LOVE
A SLAP WITH A HAND UNGLOVED
DOES THE LIGHT EVER REALLY REACH THE WEAK
WHO MOVES HER LIPS WHEN SHE ATTEMPTS TO SPEAK

SHE'S THE WEAPON AND THE INJURY, READ HER BOOK
OH HOW SHE LOVES TO PLAY WITH ME…THAT SUBTLE LOOK

INTO THE MIX AS THEY SAY…. SPIN IT AROUND
ALL THE TIMES I USED TO PRAY…MY WINGS NEVER LEFT THE GROUND

A MISSED PAYMENT OF LOVE
A BAND-AID WITHOUT BLOOD
ALL OF HER SICKENED TIES
ALL OF HER WICKED LIES

DECISION IS NOT HER SISTER, FRIEND OR JURY
HER PROBLEMS STAND IN CONCRETE, THE ANSWERS COME IN NO HURRY

IS THE VIEW FROM A GOLDEN CELL...GOLDEN
THE THOUGHTS SHE TELLS...THEY WERE SOLD WHEN

LOVE AT FIRST SITE
(SUPPLEMENTALS)

VERSE II

I dreamed of you later that same night
As I lay in bed your color broke the light
If I'd bit down through the usual fear
Caught you at the door, you'd be right here, Baby…

Is it all just wait and see,…will my heart someday return to me
I'm getting older and I never can break free
Company's a stranger, loves still foreign to me

VERSE III

Circumstance,…it came to pass
Like a schoolboy, I just ditched your class
Indecision…broken-fantasy, well…
Did you really mean that much to me, Maybe…

Pocket-searching for my keys and my pride, never really opened the feelings inside
Been to the edge, now I know that I've died
Swallowing the thoughts of you is just willed suicide

POEMS

(POSITIVE)

SHE

SHE WALKS THROUGH THE NIGHT
BACKLIT BY CANDLELIGHT

SHE COMES TO ME WITHOUT RESERVATION
OFFERS ME EMANCIPATION...FROM THE WORLD

SHE CAN PRY THE TIGHTLY SEALED OPEN
GIVES ME AIR WHEN I AM CHOKIN'

LIKE A STONE I SINK IN HER SEA
LIKE WINE SHE DRINKS ME
HER HANDS SEEM TO HOLD MY REVERENCE
HER HEART HOUSES LOVE'S PERMANENCE

SHE MENDS MY SOUL WHEN IT BEGINS TO FRAY
PROMISES THE SUN WILL RISE ANOTHER DAY

SHE'S RICH SOIL TO A FARMER'S LIPS
ALCOHOL THAT SHOULD ONLY BE SIPPED

A RAINBOW THAT NEVER NEEDS THE SUN
A PHENOMENON

SHE UNFOLDS MY SOUL LIKE A WRINKLED BILL
IS THE ONLY ONE WHO CAN BREAK MY WILL
SHE'LL HOLD THE LADDER WHEN I REACH FOR THE SKY
STEAL FOR ME WHAT I CAN'T BUY

SHE'S HUNGRY TONIGHT
HER EYES…HER APPETITE

HER LOVE IS LIKE A CANNIBAL
SHE FEEDS ON ME LIKE AN ANIMAL

SHE TIGHTENS THE REINS IF I GET TOO WILD
WHEN IN NEED, CRADLES ME LIKE A CHILD

FILLS MY PEN WITH INSPIRATION
LEADS ME NOT INTO TEMPTATION
SHE IS THE CORNERSTONE OF MY WALL
SHE IS MY ALL

THANK YOU

MY HEART,…OPEN IN YOUR HAND
ONCE DESERT, MY FEELINGS NOW GROW ON FERTILE LAND

IN MY ESTIMATION, THIS IS A SALVATION DAY
GOD HAS SENT TO ME HIS TRANSLATION PATHWAY

MY GRIEF WAS ONCE TIED TO SUNKEN SHIPS
MY BELIEF REVIVED NOW CLINGS TO YOUR LIPS

SUCH A SCULPTURE ARE YOU, STONE COULD NOT COPY
IF YOU WANTED ME TO CURTAIN THE SUN, NOTHING WOULD STOP ME

YOUR WORDS…A ROBIN'S SONG FILLING THE SKY
YOUR THOUGHTS…THE TREES FROM WHICH THE BIRDS FLY

I ONCE THOUGHT THE PAGES OF LIFE WERE STUCK TOGETHER
NOW I REALIZE THAT THE BOOKS ARE SEASONS AND THE CHAPTERS WEATHER

I LOVE YOU MY BUTTERFLY, RED ROSE AND LOYAL LIGHT
THANK YOU FOR THE WINGS, THE COLOR AND FOR CHASING-OFF THE NIGHT

SEEING YOU

SEEING YOU, I CAN'T LOOK AROUND ANYMORE…
SHOES HELD FIRMLY BY THE GROUND, MY EYES NEVER BORE

YOU'RE A SIGHT THAT'S BRIGHT…A COMET'S TAIL
I HOLD MY MEMORIES TO THE LIGHT AND RECALL ALL DETAIL

A SPANISH HAZE HANGS SOFTLY AROUND YOUR LIPS
…AN IRISH DAZE AS I DRINK YOU IN HURRIED SIPS

WHETHER A NEWS HEADLINE OR A CHURCH BELL CHIME…YOU MOVE ME
I READ YOUR STORIES AND LISTEN TO YOUR HEART'S GLORIES TENDERLY

LET COMFORT STRETCH IT'S WINGS AND WE'LL BOTH TAKE FLIGHT…
AS WE SCULPT A UNION THAT COVERS US FROM ANY OUTSIDE SIGHT

A MOMENT WITH YOU

YOUR LOVE IS MY ROSE, INTENSITY THE COLOR RED
THOSE PEDAL-LIPS MY SKIN'S CLOTHES, THEY SPRINGBOARD WORDS TO MY HEAD

IN THE LIGHT I MOVE WITH YOU…
IN THE DARK I IMPROVE THE VIEW

I FLY ACROSS YOUR COUNTRY AS IF EFFORT DOESN'T LIVE
I HOLD TIGHT TO PASSION AS IT FASTENS ITSELF TO THE GESTURES YOU GIVE

OTHER THAN AIR, YOU'RE THE ONE THING I MUST BREATHE
WITHOUT CARE, I SINK TO YOUR DEPTHS…YOUR AFFECTIONS I SLEEP BENEATH

I LOVE YOU, HAVE ALWAYS LOVED YOU AND WILL LOVE YOU FOREVER…
NO ONE ABOVE YOU, THIS TIE IS TIED AND IN NO WAY WILL IT SLIP OR SEVER

WHY

THE CHANGE OF TINT WHEN I KISS HER LIPS
THE BALANCE OF EVERYTHING NO LONGER TIPS

FLASHING LIGHTS AND SPINNING CIRCLES DIZZY ME
SHORE-SIDE…I'M ASKED TO WALK INTO HER SEA

SHE SEEPS UNDERGROUND, NO DROUGHT, GRASS GREEN
NO CALL FOR A WAY OUT, IT NOW SEEMS SO ROUTINE

SHE LIVES HER LIFE THE WAY SHE FEELS…
SHE GIVES TO ME THE DAYS AND NEVER STEALS

DIRECTING TRAFFIC IN MY HEAD, SHE JAILS ALL FEAR
WALLED BY HER TOUCH, MY RESCUE, MY DEAR

HER LIFE, A PLATTER OF PLEASURE TO TASTE
WHY DID SHE CHOOSE ME TO GUARD THIS SACRED PLACE

GOSPEL

HE IS OUR SAVIOR….
HIS BLOOD WASHES ALL THAT WE ONCE WERE

NO WORDS CAN DESCRIBE THE ACTIONS OF THE LORD
NO HUMAN-BEING CAN ESCAPE HIS SWORD

HE IS THE SPACE IN OUR HEARTS OF WHICH WE ALL YEARN
THE NEED TO SEEK-OUT HIS WISDOM, TO UNDERSTAND…TO LEARN

ALMIGHTY COME TO ME WHEN I PUSH YOU AWAY
DETOUR MY PATH WHEN I BEGIN TO STRAY
SHOW TO ME THE LESSONS OF YOUR WILL
BRIDLE MY SINFUL SOUL AND MAKE IT STILL

I FEEL YOUR POWER AND IT MAKES ME STRONG…
I NEVER REALIZED IT WAS THERE ALL ALONG

PRAYER, MY TELEPHONE TO YOU
THERE'S NEVER A BUSY SIGNAL OR CALL THAT DOESN'T GET THROUGH

PLEASE MAKE ROOM AT MY TABLE TO SEAT YOUR CHAIR
BLOOD TO WINE AND BODY TO BREAD, THE FEAST WE SHARE

AS I BOW, HUMBLE ME
AS I WALK, STAND BESIDE ME
LET ME LOVE MY ENEMY…
LET ME SHOW TO OTHERS WHAT SIGHT YOU GIVE TO SEE

THE DAY IS NEAR WHEN ALL WILL BE CALLED TO REJOIN THEE
A DAY WHEN THE SAVED ARE RECLAIMED SPIRITUALLY

REMEMBER THE PAIN ENDURED AS HE WAS NAILED TO THE TREE
WITHOUT OUR FATHER'S LOVE WE WOULD HAVE NEVER BEEN SIN FREE

SPREAD THE WORD AND KEEP THE FAITH ON FIRE
LET YOUR ACTIONS REVEAL WHO IS TRULY YOUR SIRE

NEXT

INSPIRATION COVERS ME LIKE A WAVE
WE ALL HAVE SOME CAUSE WE WISH TO SAVE

I KNOW I'M NOT WHOM I'M SUPPOSED TO BE
I LONG TO BE SOMEONE ELSE, BUT WHO IS HE

I LIVE IN THE LAND OF RICH SOIL, PRAYER AND JESUS
IS IT WRONG TO FEED ON THE THINGS THAT PLEASE US

MY LIFE ISN'T MINE, I THINK THAT ALL THE TIME
PRISONERS AREN'T ALWAYS GUILTY OF A CRIME
NIGHTFALL DECEIT CAN OVERCOME WITHOUT WARNING
SOMETIMES I MUST REPENT IN THE EARLY LIGHT OF MORNING

SUCCESS SWIMS ON TOP OF PERSEVERANCE AND CHANCE
DISAPPOINTMENT, A STONE TIED TO THE ANKLE OF CIRCUMSTANCE

WHAT'S YOUR OBJECT OF SECURITY
DOES IT HELP YOU MAINTAIN SIMPLICITY

I DON'T KNOW WHAT I'M IN, JUST WHERE I'VE BEEN
LIFE SOMETIMES FEELS LIKE SALT IN SEVERED SKIN

THE HEART IS WHERE THE HEAD BELONGS
TO SING IS TO KNOW THE LYRICS IN SONGS
I WILL ACHIEVE WHAT'S INSIDE OF ME…
I MUST NEVER GIVE-UP, NEVER FAIL TO BELIEVE

EVERY AUTHOR WANTS TO BE SUPERMAN
EVERY MUSICIAN…BOB DYLAN

I JUST WANT TO BE SOMEWHAT SATISFIED
DON'T NEED TO REACH THE MOUNTAIN-TOP, JUST WANT TO SCALE THE SIDE

OH…HANDS DON'T FORGET TO GRASP…THEN SEIZE
ALL OF LIFE'S EXTENDED POSSIBILITIES

REWIND

TO BE UNKIND…
THAT IS THE WORST STATE OF MIND

TO IGNORE THOSE WHO HAVE BECOME OLD
TO DIVORCE THOSE WITH A RING OF GOLD

TO WHISPER WHIPPING WORDS
TO STEAL FLIGHT FROM BIRDS

THE ROPE SO OFTEN GETS TWISTED
WHEN THE FEELING OF HOPE IS NO LONGER LISTED
IS A CENTERED-FOCUS OF COMPASSION REAL
OR IS GOODNESS A NEEDLE WE SHOULDN'T FEEL

TO SEVER TIES THAT BIND
TO ENCOURAGE THE BANEFUL THOUGHTS IN YOUR MIND

TO STEAL CANDY FROM A BABY
TO TELL A FRIEND IN NEED…MAYBE

TO ISOLATE YOUR SELF FROM THE WORLD
TO BURN THE FLAGS YOU ONCE FURLED

HITTING ANOTHER LEAVES YOU EXPOSED
IT OPENS DOORS THAT SHOULD REMAIN CLOSED
YOU SHOULDN'T BURN THAT WHICH BURNS YOU
DO UNTO OTHERS AS YOU WOULD HAVE THEM DO TO YOU

TO VIEW TRAGEDY AND NOT LEND A HAND
TO RAPE THE WORLD AND ITS LAND

TO DISOBEY YOUR PARENTS
TO IGNORE THE THINGS THAT MAKE SENSE

TO HARBOR SHIPS FROM OTHER PORTS
TO RESORT TO WICKEDNESS OF ALL SORTS

TO BE UNKIND…
THAT IS THE WORST STATE OF MIND
STOP…REWIND

ANYTHING (1)

I REALIZED TODAY…TO BE ANYTHING, YOU CAN'T CONCENTRATE ON EVERYTHING
SO THE ANGELS SING…

LIVING LIFE IN A LOOSE-LEAF FOLDER
HOPING TO GET TORN-OUT BEFORE I GET OLDER

I NEED A SUBSTITUTE, NEW STIMULI TO BOOT
SOMEWHERE TO RUN, TO CHEAT LIFE, TO RE-ROOT

A HURRIED SITUATION…
PRODUCES ONLY ONE KIND OF REVELATION…
IT IS BETTER TO ENJOY EACH PASSING DAY
RATHER THAN PUT-OFF HAPPINESS BY GETTING IN THE WAY

LIFE'S MIXTURE SEEMS TO HAVE SETTLED AT THE BOTTOM OF MY GLASS
THE WET-RING LEAVES A CIRCLE AROUND MY BRAIN AS I STIR THE MASS

HOW MANY CUPS OF COFFEE DO YOU DRINK TO BE GLAD
I SOMETIMES NEED TEN TO VALVE-FILL MY HEART WHEN SAD

WHEN YOU EAT YOUR BREAKFAST WITH CHAMPIONS, SIT-UP STRAIGHT
HOLD ONTO TRUSTED COMPANIONS, ATTACH THEM TO REASON WHEN BOXING FATE

EVERYONE NEEDS DISAPPOINTMENT TO KICK THEM IN THE ASS
EVEN IF YOU ONLY BRUSH ITS SHOULDER WHEN YOU ATTEMPT TO DETOUR OR PASS
TO BLAZE, TO LIGHT-UP QUICKLY THEN SMOLDER
TO MAINTAIN, TO STAY THE SAME, JUST TURN-UP THE FLAME AS YOU GET COLDER

CENTER YOUR ENERGY AROUND PLAUSIBILITY
REFRAIN FROM UNBELIEVING ACTIVITY

DON'T SPEND ALL OF YOUR TIME SAVING CAB-FARE CASH
YOU'LL ONLY DIE A WEALTHY SHELL, AN URN FOR UNFERTILE ASH

I REALIZED TODAY…TO BE ANYTHING, YOU CAN'T CONCENTRATE ON EVERYTHING
SO THE ANGELS SING…

SURVIVAL

SOMETIMES LIKE WOOD, I APPEAR HARD
ALTHOUGH POROUS, MY RINGS ARE GREEN…NOT CARVED

MY PURPOSE IS THE PURSUIT OF FINDING ME
TO BE IN THE SUNLIGHT OR SHADOWS…A LOCK OR THE KEY

FULL COLOR IN MY HEAD OFTEN PRINTS BLACK
THE SCOPE OF MY WORTH I CONSISTANTLY ATTACK

TO BE GREAT, I'M LEARNING YOU MUST KNOW THE SOUL
DISAPPOINTMENT CAN MAKE YOU DROWN…PUSH YOU INTO A SINKHOLE

BUT, I'M BEGINNING TO FIND THE HEAT TO KEEP WARM
THE POWER WITHIN MY REACH TO CREATE OR DENY ANY STORM

THE BASE OF ANY WALL SHOULD BE YOU
THE BRICKS YOUR FAMILY AND FRIENDS…DESIRE THE GLUE

HOW THE WORLD SEES ME, SHOULD THAT BE A CONCERN
IF ONE BECOMES A VIEWED SUBJECT DOES ONE RETURN

CAN YOU BE PUSHED FORWARD AND STILL REMAIN PURE
CAN YOU DANCE WITH WEALTH AND WEAR A BLUE COLLAR

JUST FOR YOU

TIME EXPLODES IN MY HANDS…PIECES EVERYWHERE
YOU'RE PIECE 147…HEAVEN, PLEASE SHARE

I'D LIKE TO HAVE COFFEE IN YOUR WHITE FORD
…LIKE TO PLAY CHESS ON YOUR GAMEBOARD

TO BRING FLOWERS TO YOUR BACK DOOR…
TO OPEN LOCKS THAT I COULDN'T BEFORE

WANT TO SPEAK SPANISH IN YOUR EAR
GRAB YOUR HAND, WALK THE WRONG SIDE OF FEAR

TRAVEL TO THE PLACE WHERE SHELTER SHIELDS
RUN IN COTTON CLOTHES THROUGH OUR MEMORY FIELDS

KINDLE A FIRE THAT IGNITES A SATURDAY NIGHT
WATCH OUR LOVE BURN BEYOND SIZE OR HEIGHT

MOVE YOU INTO ANOTHER MIND STATE…
WILL YOU BUILD NEXT TO ME MY NEIGHBOR, MY SOULMATE

THOUGHTS TODAY

SHE GIVES ME CREDIT WHEN I'M IN DOUBT
HER LOVE'S THE ONE THING I CAN'T LIVE WITHOUT

LIKE BATTER SHE MIXES ME TIL' I'M BEATEN
LIKE RAW MEAT I'M COOKED THEN OFTEN EATEN

SHE'S A TOPPING TO SWEETEN ANY DESSERT
SHE'S THE TOPSOIL THAT BLANKETS THE HURT

WHEN TIME PASSES SHE SPINS THE SECOND HAND
WITH NOTHING IN MY POCKET...I'M THE RICHEST MAN

SHE'LL PATCH THE WONDER AND THE CREEPING FEAR
AND LIKE THE RAIN SHE MAKES THE THUNDER REAPPEAR

A LIFE BOAT TO MY SINKING ARM
SHE CAN ALWAYS EXPOSES THE BOY BEHIND THE CHARM

HER BEAUTY FILLS THE HOLES IN MY HEART-SEAMS
HER SUBTLE WAYS ADD THE COLOR TO MY BLACKENED DREAMS

A TELEPHONE THAT IS JUST A RECEIVER
SHE'S THE TRUTH THAT MAKES ME A NEW BELIEVER

NEVER A NEGATIVE THOUGHT WHEN THINKING OF HER WAYS
ONLY BRIGHT SUNSHINE AND CHAMPAIGN KISSES FOUND NEXT TO BETTER
DAYS

YOUR HAND

TO TOUCH YOUR HAND IS TO COMPLETE CIRCLE-LOVE
A SIMPLE BAND, ONE OF NEED, BUT NOT NEEDY OF

A PLACE CREATED BY MOST DANCING LIGHTS
WITH SHADOWS IN RESERVE FOR THOSE LATE NIGHTS

WE WALK THEN RUN TO THE EDGE OF THE SEA
MY HAND NEXT TO YOUR HAND, OUR BODIES CUT THE WATER EVENLY

OUR VIEW

HEY…DON'T CHECK OUR ALTITUDE
LET'S JUST FLY AND SOAR INTO BLUE

WITH SECURE WINGS AND SURE SKIES…
WE CAN SAIL INTO THE CORNER OF LOVE'S EYES

TO TASTE THE WIND AND TO LEAVE OUR SKIN
WE PRESS THE EDGE, DIVE, THEN ONCE MORE BEGIN

A CALLING THAT BRINGS US OVER ANY RIDGE…
…THE WHISPERING OF SPIRITS TRYING TO BRIDGE

A HEART-CALM SILENCE IS THE PEACE WE'VE FOUND
A TOUCH, A NOD, HEIGHTS SO FAR ABOVE THE GROUND

AN EXPERIMENT TURNED JOURNEY, NOW A LIFESTYLE
GOD'S SHOULDER-TAP…EXPLOSIVE, A PRELUDE TO A SMILE

WE STAY CERTAIN IN THIS LATHER, BODIES CLEAN…
WASHING AWAY PAST DAYS AND THE DIRT IN-BETWEEN

NO MORE FEAR

I HAVE SEEN THE SOFTER SIDE OF A WOMAN-TODAY
IT WAS HIDDEN BEFORE…BEHIND THE SMOKE AND THE GRAY

THERE ARE SOME THINGS YOU HAVE TO GAMBLE-YES
I'VE THROWN SOME DICE, LAID SOME CARDS…I CONFESS

BUT THIS TIME IT'S ALL SO CLEAR
THESE FEELINGS JUST DON'T DISAPPEAR
YOU'VE GOT MY SHELTER, I WANT TO BUILD HERE
STAY WITH ME, THE PAST IS KILLED–NO MORE FEAR
…NO MORE FEAR

"PERFECT" USED TO BE THE WORD IN MY HEAD
NOW I STAND IN BEAUTY'S HANDS…OVER-FED

DON'T YOU KNOW–YOU MOVE ME, KNOCK ME DOWN…
I'M YOUR BEGGAR-BOY, A TOURIST IN YOUR WORLD–SPUN AROUND

AGAIN, YOU REACH FOR ME.
MY HEART NOW DRIED BY YOUR SUN, NO MORE SEA
THE CLOUDS THEY SWIRL AND FORGET TO TEAR
STAY WITH ME, TAKE MY HAND DEAR
…NO MORE FEAR

MY LOVE

MY LOVE ISN'T A DEMONSTRATION…
IT'S A PROMISE OF MY DEDICATION

IT'S HAVING AND HOLDING YOUR ATTENTION
THE PASSING OF THOUGHTS TO YOU WITHOUT MENTION

IT'S AN OPEN LINE STRAIGHT TO OPPORTUNITY
A WINDOW WHICH LEADS TO FUTURE UNITY

MY LOVE IS RESTING ON YOUR ANGEL WINGS
A STEAM THAT RISES OVER WHAT PASSION BRINGS

IT'S A ROADWAY TO JUST ONE PARKING SPACE
AN EXPLOSION OF ENERGY GUIDED BY TEACHING GRACE

IT'S A TREE THAT GROWS TO BECOME ROOTED DEEP
A BELIEF WHICH PILLOWS YOUR HEAD WHEN ASLEEP

MY LOVE BOARDERS ON THE COUNTRIES YOU RULE
A NOTE ON YOUR LOCKER THAT YOU READ AFTER SCHOOL

IT'S A COAL IN THE FIRE THAT WILL HOWL AND HISS
AN ICE CUBE IN THE DRINK YOUR LIPS LIKE TO KISS

IT'S THE HUNGER THAT BUILDS WHEN LEFT WITHOUT
THE WATER THAT MIXES ANY SEDIMENT OF DOUBT

MY LOVE IS THE BACKGROUND TO YOUR AMAZING VIEW
MY LOVE IS SIMPLY…A DEEP BREATH OF YOU

WOMAN

CIRCLE-SPINS ON A CIRCULAR EARTH
SHE'S RISING ABOVE HER FORMER WORTH

COMING INTO A FEELING THAT WAS ABSENT BEFORE
SHE'LL NEVER HIT THE CEILING…NEVER CLOSE THE DOOR

A WOMAN'S HEART, A WOMAN'S HAND
SHE'S CRAFTING HER ART, STARTING TO UNDERSTAND

LETTING HER ROOTS GRASP A NEW ROCK-BED
HER PETALS UNFOLDING, REACHING THE ONCE DEAD

A TRAPEZE ARTIST…SHE KNOWS ABOUT NETS
THIS TIME CIRCUMSTANCE HAS HER RAISING HER BETS

MANY THOUGHTS ABOUT THE HUNGER INSIDE
SHE WANTS A FULL STOMACH, NO EMPTINESS WILL BIDE

A BEAUTY WHO ADDS COLOR TO AN EMPTY SPACE
REMARKABLE ARE HER FEATURES OF CRADLED GRACE

HOPING HER CLIMB LEADS TO GREATER VIEWS
SHE TAKES HER GLASSES TO SEE THE MANY HUES

ROBBER

LIKE A THIEF, I SOMETIMES STEAL FROM YOU
WHEN I RETURN TO THE CRIME YOUR GUARDS PATROL BY TWO

AS I TRAMPLE YOUR GARDEN AND BURN YOUR FIELDS…
I CAUSE YOU TO REINFORCE YOUR WALLS AND SHIELDS

I DON'T MEAN TO SOUND YOUR ALARMS OR FIRE MY GUN
I JUST WANT TO ROB YOUR HEART…THEN RANDOMLY RUN

YOUR TREASURE IS THE BELIEF AND TRUST YOU GIVE TO ME
IF I BURY OUR WEALTH I LOSE THE WARMTH THAT COULD BE

SO LOCK ME UP, BUT DON'T EVER LET ME CONVICT YOU
FOR I LOVE YOUR PRISONS, MY LIFE SENTENCE AND THE THOUGHT OF NO RESCUE

OPEN ARMS

I GUESS I NEVER KNEW HOW DEEP LOVE COULD GO
SOMEHOW I KNEW YOU WERE THE ONE I WOULD SHOW

AS I RECEIVE THE GIFTS YOU GIVE...I WONDER WHAT CAN I AWARD
ARE THE RETURNS I SEND REFLECTING THE FEELINGS I RUN TOWARD

SUBTLETY...SUCH A SOFT LIGHT YOU CAST ON ME
YOU MAKE ME BELIEVE IN WHAT I IMAGINE WILL BE

I SEE YOU BUT I STILL CAN'T UNDERSTAND...
WHY DID GOD REACH OUT AND GIVE ME YOUR HAND

I 'M UNDER CONSTRUCTION SINCE YOU KNOCKED ME DOWN
YOUR SPIRIT ALWAYS ABOVE ME AS I'M SPINNING TOWARDS THE GROUND

A WATERFALL OF EMOTION RAINS ONTO ME...
AS I BATHE IN YOUR SEA OF EXTENDED CERTAINTY

THE FIRES OF PASSION THAT ONCE EMPTIED ONTO THE WORDS I SAID
NOW HIGHLIGHT THE THOUGHTS TO BE NEAR YOU IN MY HEAD

I STEP INTO THE WHITE SUNLIGHT WHERE SHADOWS ONCE CAST...
I SUDDENLY REMEMBER HOW TO GET BACK TO THE PLACE WE LEFT LAST

WITH MY ARMS STRETCHED FROM HERE TO THERE...
I REACH FOR YOUR HEART AND AM GRANTED MY PRAYER

ANGEL-SPACE

LIKE TWO BIRDS IN FLIGHT, OUTLINED BY THE SUN…
OUR SHADOWS CAST AGAINST THE CLOUDS AS ONE

SEE THE SKY BENEATH HER SMILE, SUNSET RED
I PRAY TO GOD IN THE CHURCH AISLE…NOTHING SAID

WE PLAY LIKE STREET-CHILDREN…WITHOUT CARE
OUR SEASONS WARM, OUR LOVE A SCHOOL-YARD DARE

OPEN IS THE DOORWAY TO HER THOUGHTS UNTOLD
CLOSED ARE HER EMOTIONS REGARDING THE COLD

THE FEELING OF FOREVER WHEN CLOSENESS APPEARS
…LANDSCAPED VIEWS SHAPED BY A LOVE THAT CLEARS

SAY YES TO THE FORTUNES THAT NOW LAY AT OUR FEET
THE PLEASURES OF LIFE HAVE ALL PARKED ON ONE STREET

LOVE, STAY NEXT TO ME LIKE A SHEPHERD TO SHEEP
SHOW ME THE DAYLIGHT BEYOND THE SHADOWED DEEP

IN THE ARMS OF PEACE WE CAN LEARN TO KNOW GOD'S GRACE
EVERYTHING TURNING AROUND US, YOU AND I IN ANGEL-SPACE

GLASS

LOVE SHOULD BE AS CLEAR AS GLASS…
MOLDED TO CATCH ALL, HANDLED TO PASS

ABLE TO MAGNIFY THAT WHICH IS SMALL
HARD ENOUGH NOT TO SHATTER IF IT WERE TO FALL

TO WITHSTAND HIGH HEAT OR ICY COLD
DECORATIVE YET SIMPLE, NOT SILENT OR BOLD

EASY TO CLEAN IF EVER STAINED
EASY TO RESTORE IF EVER PAINED

NEVER TOO SHARP WHEREAS CUTS WOULD OCCUR
SMOOTH BUT NOT SLIPPERY, THOUGHT-OUT BUT NEVER SURE

REFLECTIVE, IF NECESSARY EVEN MIRRORED…
TO BE HANDLED WITH CARE BUT NEVER FEARED

A CUP, TELEVISION SCREEN OR DISPLAY CASE…
LOVE, LIKE GLASS ACCOMMODATES MANY TASTES

AFTER HOURS

SILENCE BECOMES SURRENDER AS WE LAY SIDE BY SIDE
TOGETHER WE RUN FROM THE TIME, HOPING TO SOMEHOW HIDE

I LOVE THE DARKNESS WHEN MY EYES BEGIN TO CLOSE
THE FEEL OF SKIN...YOUR LIPS LIKE THE PEDALS OF A ROSE

THE SHEETS THAT WE SHARE CAN READILY ACCEPT OR DISMISS
AS A SHELTER OR WALL THEY CAN HONOR OR REJECT ANY WISH

TO MOVE IS TO TURN AS YOU TURN...FEELING MY HEART SLIP
I SWEAT, THEN BURN, AS YOUR CUP HOUSES THE FLAVORS I SIP

YOUR EYES...THE FOCUS OF MY CARE AND OBLIGATION
PERMANENTLY ENTAGLED IN YOUR STARE...I'M IN NEED OF NO OTHER SALVATION

ANYTHING (2)

SEPARATED BY DISTANCES WHICH MEASURE THE HEART
I AM SO INCLINED TO FINISH WHATEVER I START

I'LL BUY NEW SHOES IF THEY HELP ME RUN TO YOU
SELL MY IDENTITY TO BECOME ONE VERSUS TWO

ASK ROYALTY TO EXPENSE MY TRIPS TO PLACES YOU GO
HOLD THE WEATHER HOSTAGE IF THE WIND AND RAIN WERE TO BLOW

SPEND THE NIGHT IN A LION'S DEN…
GET SENT TO JAIL ONLY TO ESCAPE AGAIN

RUN INTO TRAFFIC TO STOP THE CARS
GOT TO MEDICAL SCHOOL SO I COULD HEAL YOUR SCARS

TAKE A RISK EVEN IF TINTED WITH DOUBT
DO ANYTHING FOR YOUR LOVE BECAUSE I CAN'T LIVE WITHOUT

UNTITLED

TIME…IT SWIMS FOREVER IN YOUR EYES
…I REACH FOR YOU WHEN THE RIVERS RISE

SO MUCH WATER THE BANKS ALWAYS OVERFLOW
MY AIR IS YOUR AIR, TWICE USED BEFORE LETTING GO

SUCH A POETIC PEACE YOU BRING TO THIS PLACE
I BELONG TO THE WARMTH THAT I SEE IN YOUR FACE

YOU'RE A TRAIN CRASH TO MY HEART…MY SENSES DERAIL
A GUNSHOT THAT AIDS ROBBERY…A THIEF I CAN'T JAIL

LIKE A BRICK SEALED IN CEMENT…I'M LEFT WITH ONLY PRIOR INTENT
NO DOUBTS OR PROJECTED FALLS…ALWAYS SECURED BY THIS ONE MOMENT

INTRODUCED TO THE NOVELTY OF YOU BY THE STARS ABOVE
MELTED, MOLDED, HAMMERED THEN TWICE-FOLDED BY THIS LOVE

PERMANENT PASSION A GAME PLAN TO GRASP AND KEEP
YOUR TOUCH…TOXIN AND YOUR ANIMATION…A SIGN OF THE ARTWORK I KEEP

I'M SO DISPLACED WITH YOUR MARTINI MOVEMENTS…
HOW YOUR WORDS WARM LIKE FABRIC IN MY ABSENCE

A FIXATION OF COMMITMENT AT UNCALCULATED COST
A MAGNET PULLING INVISIBLY…A MAP WHICH GUIDES WHEN LOST

OH, TO BE THE GROUND AT YOUR FEET…FEELING THE WEIGHT OF YOUR INDUCEMENT
WHEN TOUCHING YOUR HAND…THE MARRIAGE OF SKIN, EXCITEMENT WITH SCENT

I LOVE YOU 'CAUSE I WANT TOO, NOT BECAUSE YOU HAUNT ME THROUGH
I LOVE YOU 'CAUSE I'M SPUN-AROUND, NOW LET ME BE BURIED IN THIS HAPPI-
NESS I'VE
FOUND

POEMS

(NEGATIVE)

OTHER

LOVE, IT HURTS...I'M HURT
BITTER TASTE, MUDDY FACE...I KISS THE DIRT

GOD HELP ME TO BE FIRM BUT SENSITIVE
LET ME MEET SOMEONE THAT WANTS TO LIVE

RELIEVE MY PRIVATE, PIERCING-PAIN
UPLIFT MY SOUL THEN LET ME MAINTAIN

YOU GO UP THE STAIRS AND I GO DOWN
WHEN CLIMBING LOVE...YOU NEED RAILINGS AROUND

SOMETIMES SUGAR BUT SOMETIMES SALT
NO DIFFERENCE IN APPEARANCE...ONLY THE PRESENTATION OF FAULT

YOU KNOW THAT I STILL GET YOUR JUNK MAIL
YOU'RE NOT THE ONLY ONE WHO'S TRIED TO SELL ME THIS SALE

IS IT BETTER NOW IN THE FREE, OPEN SPACE
ARE THERE WIDER, WARMER FEELINGS TO EMBRACE

SIMPLE SYMBOLS PLAYED YOUR THEATRICAL THEME...
HAPPINESS, WASN'T ALWAYS THE SUBJECT OF THE ACTED SCENE

WILL I OVERCOME SHADOWS...FREQUENTLY CAST
STEP INTO THE LIGHT OF MY GAME-BOARD PAST

ONLY CERTAIN TREES BEAR FRUIT TO EAT
YOUR WAYS WERE SEEDED WITH ONLY DECEIT

HE

HE GOT CAUGHT IN A BACKLASH
EMPTY-HANDED WITHOUT CASH

HE'S IN BATTER-MODE, WANTS TO HIT EVERYTHING IN SIGHT
SOMEONE STOLE THE LEAD IN HIS MOVIE TITLED…"SPITE"

WEEKEND DRINKS AND SMILES DON'T CHANGE HIS CIRCUMSTANCE
HE STILL MAINTAINS THE SAME HAIRCUT, WEARS THE SAME PANTS

HIS BRAIN ENGINES HIS CIVIL WAR STATE
SWALLOWED SINS NOW ACHE…CAN HE REGURGITATE
WHEN DID HE ADJOIN HIMSELF WITH THIS CONFESSIONAL DATE
WHY DOES HE CARE WHAT COURT JUDGES HIS FATE

SICK OF BREAKFAST WITH DISEASED EMOTIONS
HIS SOUL MUST RISE FROM THE DUST OCEANS

HE'S GOT DOUBTFUL CONFIDENCE
PAIN THE PILLS CAN'T QUENCH

HANDS KNOT-TIED TO A PULSE THAT DIED
SERVITUDE TO A SENTIMENTAL BRIDE

PAGES WILL ALWAYS TURN IN THE WIND
THE HEADLINES WILL ALWAYS TELL US WHO SINNED
DAYS SIGNIFY THE WEAK
HOW DOES ONE ALTER THE COMFORTABLE AND BECOME UNIQUE

HE NEEDS A STEAM TO RELEASE THE SIN
PATIENCE…TO UNWRINKLE HIS SKIN

HIS CONSCIOUS WILL SOMETIMES CANCEL
ALL OF THE EMOTIONS THAT DON'T FULFILL

LITTLE RED MEN ON EACH SHOULDER
THEY TELL HIM HE'S TIRED AND GETTING OLDER

HALF-EMPTY

SOMETIMES I FEEL DEAD
HEART AND MIND…UNWED

THOUGHTS INDEPENDENT OF FEELING
SCARS INCAPABLE OF HEALING

WE ALL WADE IN SIN
I FLOAT TO THE TOP THEN SINK BACK IN

VACANCY TAKES RESIDENCY IN MY EYES
MY CONFIDENCE, WHAT HAPPENED TO ITS SIZE
MEMORIES A DOUBLE-FEATURE IN MY CONSCIOUS
I CAN'T STOP THINKING OF THE TWO OF US

LOOKING FOR THE LINE BETWEEN GIVE AND RECEIVE
SEARCHING FOR THE FATHER THAT I CAN BELIEVE

GOT TO RUN TO AND RUN FROM THE FEELINGS IN MY HEAD
WANT TO UNDERSTAND THE TITLE OF THE BOOK I JUST READ

WHEN DO THE ELEMENTS OF FIRE NO LONGER BURN
WHEN DOES THE PALETTE TASTE THE LESSONS LEARNED

LOVE AND TEARS SEEM INTERTWINED
ANGER AND HAPPINESS BOTH EASY TO FIND
SUCH IS MY LOOK AT MORTALITY
PASS ME A DRINK TO CLARIFY REALITY

LIFE IT IS THE ULTIMATE MACHINE
LOVE, IT IS LIFE'S PULSE…INTANGIBLE…THOUGH ALWAYS SEEN

IS THERE A KEY TO BECOMING WHOLE…
FOREVER OUTSTRETCHED ARE THE ARMS OF MY SOUL

SEND ME THE PLANS FOR A NEW MAP
I'VE GOT TO CUT THROUGH THIS FASTENED GIFT WRAP

FRUSTRATION

IT'S WHEN THE TRAFFIC LIGHTS FLASH IN MORSE CODE
...WHEN THE SUN SETS TOO LOW

WHEN THE CITY BOUNDARIES ARE THE LAST NOTCH IN YOUR BELT
WHEN YOUR FEELINGS CAN'T REMEMBER WHAT IT'S LIKE TO BE FELT

THE WINTER CHILL IN THE SUMMER HEAT
THAT HEADACHE THAT SEEMS TO BE ON CONSTANT REPEAT

VIOLENCE BREEDS IN TIGHT SPACES
ONCE BORN IT FEEDS...THEN ERASES
FRUSTRATION...SOMETIMES YOUR ONLY FRIEND
OH..WHAT A ONE WAY ROAD, WHAT A DEAD END

IT'S THE STRANGERS WHO MAKE YOU MAD
FRIENDS THAT YOU WISH YOU NEVER HAD

IT'S HAVING A JOB
...BEING FORCED TO ROB

AN EMPTY CUP
ELEVATORS DOWN WHEN YOU'RE PRESSING UP

FRUSTRATION, IT FRUSTRATES
EVERY WALL IT PENETRATES
THE DOSAGE IS BIG...MOST DAYS
WILL IT PUNCTURE YOUR SKIN, HOW MANY WAYS

IT'S YOUR SOUL COLLAPSING
...MEMORY LAPSING

TRY TO KEEP YOUR MIDPOINT STABLE
EVEN WHEN YOUR HEAD HITS THE TABLE

TIME TO PRESS THE RESET
BUT NEVER TO FORGET......THIS FRUSTRATION

WEAKENED

STUPIDITY HUMBLES, IT'S A ROPE WHICH KNOTS
DO YOU LECTURE TO THE WALLS…TO THE CEMETERY PLOTS

YOU'RE SO CAUTIOUS
IT MAKES ME NAUSEOUS

YOU HAVE NO FRAMEWORK THAT CHECKS YOUR BALANCE
A MAGICIAN WITH WORDS…YOU MERELY SUSPEND YOUR TALENTS

WILL YOU EVER HAVE SOMETHING TO HOLD
OWN SCARS BIRTHED BY LABOR NOT JUST FORCED THROUGH TIME'S MOLD
IS SAFETY YOUR SKETCHED-PLAN FOR JOY
IS THE BIRTH OF YOUR SUCCESS ALWAYS HALF-DRESSED, A LITTLE BOY

YOUR GOALS ARE TO BE EXTRAORDINARILY LIKED
YOU DIVE INTO CONVERSATION UNKNOWINGLY BUT FORGET TO PIKE

STRENGTH IS SOMETHING THAT YOU CAN'T LIFT
HOPE, A RIBBON ON A UNWRAPPED GIFT

YET YOU CONTINUE TO SWIM INTO THE RIVER'S HEART
NEVER TAKING ENOUGH AIR INTO YOUR LUNGS AS YOU START

WHAT'S THE POINT OF PRODUCING THE ROUTINE
DINING ON THE FAT OF OTHERS WON'T KEEP YOU HUNGRY AND LEAN
BEGIN YOUR LIFE AGAIN, START CLEAN
DISCOVER COUNTRIES UNSEEN

YOU'RE SUCH A MINIMALIST
NEVER WILLING TO CLASP YOUR FIST

YOUR HAND ALWAYS SHAKES WHEN YOU ATTEMPT TO LEVEL
YOU'D SWEAR THAT YOUR HEARTACHE WAS CAUSED BY THE DEVIL

C'MON, RISE TO YOUR FEET…OR AT LEAST TO YOUR KNEES
DON'T YOU KNOW LIFE IS DRIVEN BY DESIRE, DISAPPOINTMENT AND SET-
BACKS YOUR ENTRY FEES

SPUN

WHEN YOU SPIN…DO YOU GRIN
WHEN YOU SEE LOVE…DO YOU FALL IN

SMOOTH TO THE TOUCH
BUT RAZOR-SHARP WHEN EXPOSED AS SUCH

OFTEN SEEN IN BLACK ON BLACK
YOU PROWL AT NIGHT BOUND FOR PREY…READY TO ATTACK

EVERYONE NEEDS TO RESET…THEIR PALATE
TO FILL THE GAPS OF NEED WITH NO REGRET
YOU HAVE ENTOMBED YOUR PAST WITH VISIONS ANEW
SHINING SUNLIGHT ONTO WALLS SHADOWED BLUE

YOU'RE A WOMAN THAT STIRS HER DRINK WITH A FORK
A CHAMPAGNE BOTTLE WITH A HALF-DIPPED CORK

YOU'RE TOLD TO STAY IN ONE LANE OF TRAFFIC…AND IN THOUGHT
IF YOU DON'T…THEY SAY YOU'LL BE AMBULANCEBROUGHT

YOU'RE SUCH A BAD APPLE, ONCE CARAMEL…NOW JUST CORE
YOU FEEL YOU MUST GAMBLE TO GAIN, LOSE TO GET MORE

RESOURCES CAN RUN DRY
DREAMS SOMETIMES DIE
YOU RESERVE NOTHING BEYOND YOUR LIPS
YOU FIRE ALL GUNS FROM THE DECKS OF YOUR SHIPS

OH…CAN'T YOU SWING WITHOUT THE NOOSE
HOW SHARP IS THAT KNIFE YOU CLAIM TO USE

FREE-FORM EXPRESSIONISM PAINTS YOU THE COLOR RED
CHANGE, YOUR TESTAMENT OF COURAGE BUILT ON A MARBLE BED

TO BLUR IS TO SHIFT AND DISTORT IN FORM
WILL YOU ALWAYS FEED ON ADVENTURE TO STAY WARM

HEADACHE

STUCK IN TRAFFIC, THEREFORE I AM
STEEL BODIES MOVE LIKE SWINE TO THEIR SLAUGHTER…TASTE THE HAM

MY FOOT TAPS TO MY BRAIN-WAVES
THAT BUMPER STICKER SHOUTS…ONLY JESUS SAVES

I FEEL THE STRUGGLE AND WEIGHT OF MY SOUL
WILL IT RETREAT WHEN I REACH MY GOAL

TOO MUCH SUNLIGHT THEY SAY WILL BLIND
TOO MANY THOUGHTS PAY RENT TO MY MIND
I OFTEN WANT TO LEAVE, BUT KNOWN DESTINATIONS DECEIVE
WHAT CAN I ACHIEVE, WHAT CAN I BELIEVE…

PAIN WILL MAKE YOUR FOCUS INTENSE
IT WILL MAKE YOU REALIZE YOUR WEAKEST DEFENSE

HELLO…MY HALO IS HOLLOW
WHEN MY HEART LEADS SHOULD MY HEAD ALWAYS FOLLOW

WILD-FIRE IN MY BLOOD
EMOTIONS OVERCOME AND OFTEN FLOOD

OH THE GRASS ISN'T GREENER
VIEWS JUST LOOK DIFFERENT CLEANER
HOLES ARE CIRCLES ON THE OUTER EDGE
BALCONIES…SPRINGBOARDS OF WHICH DREAMS CLING TO THE LEDGE

I CAN DO ANYTHING WITH A GOOD SONG BEHIND ME
LIFT A MOUNTAIN, PUNCH THE SKY, SWIM THE SEA…WHERE IS THE OPPORTUNITY

IS IT EVER THE RIGHT-TIME TO MOVE
IS IT EVER REALLY NECESSARY TO IMPROVE

I'LL SEE WHAT HAPPENS AS I STIR THE MIX
ADDING CHANGE TO THE BATTER...THROWING IT AGAINST THE WALL TO
SEE WHAT
STICKS

QUESTION

THE HEX ON THE WATCH YOU GAVE ME HAS SPLINTERED
THE LOVE WE USED TO SHARE HAS NOW CLEARLY WINTERED

CHAMPAGNE-GLASS SEEMS TO CUT THE SAME AS EVERYDAY-WARE
I'M SURE THAT YOUR EYES STILL SHOW LOVE'S TINTED–STARE

YOU USED TO BE SUCH A GRAND HIT, NOW JUST A HINT
YOUR RECORDS ONLY COLLECT DUST AND SPIN SILENT

WHAT WE HAD WAS ROADSIDE-LOVE
IT BROKE-DOWN WHEN WE BROKE-UP
ENGAGEMENT GOLD WASN'T THAT HARD TO BREAK
WAS IT REALLY A LESSON OR JUST A BIG MISTAKE

YOU THOUGHT YOU COULD FINANCE LOVE LIKE A CAR
AN APARTMENT, DINNER, SOME DRINKS IN THE BAR

OH…YOU WOVE ME LIKE A BLANKET OF COMMERCIAL COTTON
I DIDN'T KNOW IT WOULD COVER TO THE POINT OF SOON-FORGOTTEN

LIKE AN IRON YOU WANTED TO PRESS-OUT THE WRINKLES AND DEEP LINES
TOO BAD MY CLOTHES ARE STARCHED WITH YEARS OF STEADY-STRENGTH-INCLINES

SHE WOULD SAY…YOU MUST PUSH THE GAS-PEDAL TO MOVE
BUT ON THE EDGE OF DESTRUCTION…CAN ONE'S SENSES REALLY IMPROVE
AT WHAT MOMENT SHOULD I HAVE PUSHED THE BRAKE
WAS IT REALLY A LESSON OR JUST A BIG MISTAKE

DOESN'T EVERYONE WANT TO BE IN MOVIES AND IN LOVE…SHE SAID
DOESN'T THIS RIDE EVER SLOW-DOWN I THOUGHT TO MYSELF…IN MY HEAD

SUBTLE SOUNDS THAT MADE ME BREATHE EASY
AS I REMEMBERED THE TIMES WHEN SHE SELDOM PLEASED ME

I LEFT THE KEY BY THE BED NEXT TO PAST THOUGHTS OF BLUE
LOVE IS NEVER AN OPEN DOORWAY, ONLY A WINDOW TO SEE THROUGH

NEVER CHASE ANYTHING WITH AN UNBELTED-SOUL
NEVER PEEL LAYERS THAT AREN'T STABLE AND WHOLE
SERIOUS SHIFTS WILL CAUSE A FLOW OF UNWANTED INTAKE
AND YOU WILL BEGIN TO WONDER…WAS IT REALLY A LESSON OR JUST A BIG MISTAKE

DRESSED-UP

SHE HAS AN UGLY HEART…BUT IS BEAUTIFULLY DRESSED
CAPPED-WHITE TEETH…AREN'T YOU IMPRESSED

HER LOVER, SHE CALLS HIM AN AMATEUR
HE CAN'T FEEL THE PUNCH TO THE CHIN SHE'S SURE

HER HEAD CAN'T LOOK-AWAY ANYMORE
AND THE STAIRWAY TO HER TOWER NO LONGER TOUCHES THE FLOOR

NEVER ONE TO CHECK HER REAR-VIEW MIRROR
WHEN IN THE LEAD…HER FUTURE SEEMS CLEARER
SHE TRIES TO SAVE HER ATTITUDE IN A PAPER SACK
SHE ADJUSTS HER SUNGLASSES, THEN TILTS HER SEAT BACK

SHE'LL STAND ON YOU TO CATCH HER BREATH
TO FLOAT WOULD BE TO RELAX, TO LAY-DOWN…DEATH

HER TALONS PULL LOVE AS SHE GETS PUSHED AWAY
CAN'T STAND TO LOSE POSSESSIONS THAT OFTEN STRAY

CANCER TO HER IS A PENNILESS BEAU
WILL SHE EVER REALIZE…YOU'RE ONLY AS DEEP AS THE OCEANS YOU ROW

SHE'LL CLOSE YOUR HEART LIKE A EMPTY ACCOUNT
KILL YOUR HORSE IF YOU ATTEMPT TO DISMOUNT
WILL ONLY SIT THROUGH AN R-RATED PICTURE…
AND WON'T GIVE FIRST-AID UNTIL YOUR DISEASED WITHOUT CURE

VOICES SHE SAYS GUIDE HER EVERY ACTION
JEWELRY AND MONEY HER MAIN DISTRACTION

I WONDER WHAT IT'S LIKE TO FOG THE LENS
TO SIGN BLANK CHECKS WITH BLOOD-FILLED PENS

YOU CAN'T EVER COMPETE WITH HER VICIOUS VANITY
...COMPANY WITH HER IS INSISTENT INSANITY

VACATIONS TO BEVERLY HILLS
PRESCRIPTIONS...TO MANY PILLS
HAPPINESS IS ALWAYS YOUR PERCEPTION
YOUR JOURNEY FOREVER REMAINS YOUR DIRECTION

RED

SHE POUNDS HER HANDS AGAINST THE STEERING WHEEL
WONDERS IF HE KNOWS JUST HOW SHE FEELS

SHE REMEMBERS SAYING I CAN'T LOOK AT YOU
HE ALWAYS TOLD HER WHAT TO DO

SHE THINKS SILENCE OFTEN PAYS
BUT SHE KNOWS IT DOESN'T DISCRIMINATE AGAINST VERBAL HAZE

SHE LOOKED ONCE…IT WASN'T THERE
SHE LOOKED AGAIN AND IT WAS EVERYWHERE
SEE THE DISAPPOINTMENT IN HER FACE
THE LINES SHE CAN'T ERASE

SHE REMEMBERS WHEN OTHER MEN USE TO PATROL HER BORDERS
KNOWS OF A TIME WHEN THERE WERE NO COURT ORDERS

HER MIND WANTS TO RETRIEVE THE TIME LOST
SHE WANTS TO PAY FOR THE PAIN AND GET REFUNDED THE COST

SADNESS WILL BLANKET THE HEART BUT WARM IT WILL NOT
HER DESIRES LEFT TO MISFIRE AND BURN OUT HOT

CAUGHT BETWEEN BLINDNESS AND SIGHT
SEARCHING FOR ANYTHING…EXCEPT ANOTHER FIGHT
TO STRETCH IS LENGTHEN YOUR REACH
OH…WHAT YOU NEED TO LEARN BEFORE YOU CAN TEACH

TO GET KNOCKED DOWN YOU NEED TO GET UP
TO DRINK AGAIN YOU MUST AGAIN DIP YOUR CUP

SHE WILL AGAIN RISE AND FALL LIKE THE AIR IN HER CHEST
RECALLING THE MARKS RECEIVED FOR THIS TORSION TEST

ESCAPISM IS WHAT SHE WILL NEED
SOME NEW PASSION ON WHICH TO FEED

YOU

YOU, YOU'RE SO SELF-RIGHTEOUS
TEARING-UP THE BOTH OF US

NEVER WANT TO USE THE BRAKES IN YOUR MIND
THOSE GAS-PEDAL LIPS ALWAYS PUSHIN' THE RED LINE

NEED...YOUR GROWING SEED
TREE OF FRUIT OR POISON WEED
YOU WANT TO KEEP ME IN THIS HALF-SPACE
OH I WOULD LOVE TO SLAP YOUR FACE

YOU LIVE ON SATURN, IT IS CERTAIN
NO EARTHLY WOMAN, NO PERSON

WANT ME AS A SHADOW IN YOUR SUN
...IN THE SIGHTS OF YOUR GUN

YOUR WILL IS SO STRONG...
EVEN WHEN YOUR WRONG...

I'VE SEEN YOUR PEACEFULNESS DISAPPEAR
WHERE YOU HAVE GONE ISN'T REALLY CLEAR
IT'S HARD TO LOVE SOMEONE YOU HATE
I CAN'T BELIEVE I BIT THE BAIT

YOU ENTER A ROOM LIKE A TRAIN WRECK
YOUR TRACKS NEVER CHANGE DIRECTION, NOT YET

YOU CAN'T WAIT TO ORDER DISORDER
AS AVERSION CONTINUES TO CONSTRUCT YOUR BOARDER

NOTHING BUT TUNNEL VISION, MATERIAL-DROWNED
YOUR DESTRUCTION...A TEN-SECOND COUNTDOWN

YOU'RE A BAD INGREDIENT IN THIS BATTERED MIX
A SHE-SERPENT WHOM I WON'T LET FURTHER CONSTRICT
NO MORE ADHERENCE TO YOUR APPEARANCE, BE GONE
ALL THAT I'VE GIVEN TO YOU IS NOW WITHDRAWN

MISTRUST

PAIN, A ROOTED WEED WHO'S FLOWERS HAVE BLOWN AWAY
ME, THE ONE WHO BIT THE HOOK YOU BAITED…LEFT TO DECAY

NOW DOWNWARD DRIVEN BY FORCES I CAN'T SEE
I PRAY FOR SOME COMPANY

ALWAYS SEEMED TO NEED THE THOUGHT OF YOU
NEVER DOUBTED YOU NEEDED ME TOO
ARMS THAT ONCE HELD YOU NOW REPEL
I CAN'T BELIEVE HOW FAR I FELL

YOU SEEM TO BLACKEN SUNLIGHT
WHO WILL CATCH YOUR STAR WHEN IT FALLS FROM NIGHT

WHEN OPPORTUNITY KNOCKS YOU NEVER CEASE TO SEIZE
YOU JUST WRAP YOUR HANDS AROUND ITS NECK AND BEGIN TO SQUEEZE

OH…WHAT DRAINED YOU HEART.
AH…WHEN DID IT START

SILVER LINING RIPPED AWAY
I SEW MY SCARS AS THOUGHTS OF YOU REPLAY
HOW MANY DAYS WILL IT TAKE
BEFORE I RECOVER FROM THIS HEART-QUAKE

MORE THORNS THAN ROSES ARE WHAT YOU BESTOW
HIDDEN PAIN AND LUKEWARM PLEASURE IS ALL THAT YOU KNOW

WILL YOU EVER CHANGE, WILL YOU EVER CARE
WHAT WILL BECOME OF YOUR UNTANGLED SMILE AND CLINCHING STARE

I LONG FOR THE DAY WHEN IT ALL COMES FULL CIRCLE
WHEN SOMEONE BURIES YOU AT LOVE'S FUNERAL

ALWAYS SEEMED TO NEED THE THOUGHT OF YOU
NEVER DOUBTED YOU NEEDED ME TOO
ARMS THAT ONCE HELD NOW DIG DEEP
AS I CLIMB TO THE PERCH FROM WHERE I ONCE I LEAPED

RANDOM

THE WIRES GOT CROSSED IN YOUR HEAD
THOUGHTS OF TRAFFIC, RENT AND SEX COLLIDED

CAUGHT IN THE IN-BETWEEN
CONTENT WITH NOTHING SEEN

DO YOU LIKE WHAT YOU DO
DOES THE RADIO SET YOUR MOOD

LET IT GO, UNTANGLE THE UNATTAINABLE
MAKE IT ALL SO SUSTAINABLE
YOU ALWAYS WANTED TO CLIMB ON STAGE
NOW YOU'RE COMING OF AGE

YOU RIP ME UP SO NO ONE CAN READ ME
EMPTY MY CUP IN ORDER TO BLEED ME

BOUGHT WHAT YOU COULD SELL
SOLD WHAT INFORMATION YOU COULD TELL

I LOVE TO WATCH YOU IN ACTION
OH...HOW YOU LIKE THIS FLEETING INFRACTION

STRANGE DAYS, YOUR HORIZONS STOP WITH YOU
NO RAYS FROM YOUR SUN, IT'S FROZEN RESOLUTE BLUE
ENTER AT YOUR OWN RISK YOUR FOREHEAD READS
RANDOM THOUGHTS ARE ALL THAT YOU PERCEIVE

MONEY...ROOT OF ALL EVIL ANCHORS YOUR TREE OF LIFE
WHEN YOU WRESTLE WITH YOUR SOUL, DO YOU EVER GRAB THE KNIFE

YOU'RE A FULL MEAL EVEN WHEN WERE HAVING COFFEE
YOU'RE ALL-TERRAIN GEOGRAPHY

SPONTANEITY YOU NEVER LACK
TOO MANY GROCERIES FILL YOUR BROWN-PAPER SACK

IT

IT'S MORE ABOUT SUBSTANCE THAN IMAGE
HANGING ONTO NOT JUMPING OVER THE LEDGE

WHAT SEAT YOU HAVE ON THE WORLD'S TRAIN
THE TASTE OF BITTER LOVE OR SUGAR CANE

THE SCALE ON WHICH YOU WEIGH...
MONEY, BEAUTY, FAME...DISMAY

WHAT DID YOU DO WITH THE GOD-GOLD
WAS IT SPENT YOUNG, SAVED...GAMBLED

DID YOU SINK YOUR NAILS SKIN DEEP
OR WERE THEY CUT ON SOMEONE ELSE'S TEETH

AS A SHAPE DID YOU COME TO EVER EVOLVE
DID YOUR MIND MIX-IN, ESCAPE OR PROBLEM-SOLVE

IS LIFE JUST SCISSORS AND PAPER CUTS
DID YOU THREE-PIG LIVE IN GRASS, GLASS OR BRICK HUTS

THE LESSONS LEARNED...BAG-TIED OR BLACK-EYED
WHAT YOU GAVE...WAS IT SMOKE, ASH OR FIRE INSIDE

PAYMENT OF LOVE (2)

HEY,…YOU MISSED YOUR PAYMENT OF LOVE
DID YOUR FEELINGS TURN…SOMEONE GIVE YOU A SHOVE

STANDING ON THE EAST SIDE OF YOU WITHOUT THE SUN
I'M MUCH COLDER NOW, THIRD-SHELF REFRIGERATION

DOES THE LIGHT EVER REALLY REACH THE WEAK
DOES SOMEONE ELSE MOVE YOUR LIPS WHEN YOU SPEAK

ALL OF YOUR SICKENED TIES…
ALL OF YOUR WICKED LIES…

IS THE VIEW FROM A GOLDEN CELL…GOLDEN
THE THOUGHTS YOU SELDOM TELL…THEY WERE SOLD WHEN

NOW YOU'VE GONE AN OPENED A HORNET'S NEST
IF YOU THINK YOU CAN PULL ME DOWN, DON'T TAKE THIS TEST

REALITY, IT'S NOT THE COVERING, IT'S THE CORE…
A LEGALITY, THE REASON I DON'T LOVE YOU ANY MORE

WHEN YOU SPIT ON ME, YOU SHOULD HAVE SPIT TWICE
NOW THE RETURN WILL DOUBLE THAT PAYMENT PRICE

I'VE PUSHED AWAY FROM YOUR TABLE AND LEFT THE BENEFIT
I'M SO GLAD I WAS ABLE TO CLIMB OUT OF AND ESCAPE THIS PIT

TORNADO SKY AS THE STORM-CLOUDS APPEAR IN YOUR EYES
THIS GAME IS NO LONGER A TIE, YOUR HEART NOT THE SAME SIZE

COFFEE-COLORED LIES STIRRED BY YOU
NO MORE SUGAR, SOME BITTERNESS IS DUE

YOU'VE BEEN ON STAGE WAY PAST THE CURTAIN
ONE ACT TOO MANY, OVER-CONFIDENCE A CERTAIN

DON'T

DON'T EVEN LOOK AT ME…
I'LL CUT RIGHT THROUGH YOU, SLIT YOU EVENLY

I NOT HERE TO BE MEAN, BLACK OR RUDE
I'VE JUST GOT AN UNCONTROLLABLE NEW ATTITUDE

AN APPETITE TO BE MORE THAN WHAT YOU SEE
A TASTE TO BE REAL…ABSOLUTELY FREE

NEVER MIND WHAT YOU MAY HAVE SEEN BEFORE
THIS PIECE OF CLAY IS NOW MOLDED TO FIT ANY DOOR

SOMETHING OF A MYSTERY THIS NEW FOUND SPIRIT IN ME
JUST WANTED TO MAKE YOU AWARE OF MY NEW DEXTERITY

WITH A WALL OF SOUND BEHIND ME, I HIT LIKE THUNDER
I UNTIE THE ROPES THAT BIND ME, PUSH-OFF THE BRICKS I'M UNDER

YOU SEE NO ONE WILL EVER AGAIN KNOCK ME DOWN
IN ONE'S MIND ONE CAN EITHER BUILD A TINY OR LARGE TOWN

I'VE BUILT A CITY WHERE THE LIGHTS NEED ME
THE RESOURCES OF OLD NO LONGER USE DARK ENERGY

I'VE GOT A BANK, A CITY HALL AND EVEN A CASINO
I'M THE MAYOR, THE POLICE AND THE AVERAGE JOE

SPENT TOO MUCH TIME LIVING IN A MUD-HOUSE…
NOW MY MIND'S DRY AND THERE'S A DIRTY TASTE IN MY MOUTH

NEVER THOUGHT I COULD BE SENTENCED TO SLEEP
…GOT TO BREAK-FREE AND RISE ABOVE THE KNEE-DEEP

STAND NEXT TO ME AND I'LL SHARPEN ANYTHING
TALK TO ME AND I'LL MAKE THE ANGELS SING

THE SCENE HAS CHANGED, TIME TO RE-TRUST MY WAYS
STAINLESS-STEEL-CLEAN, I'M CUTTING THROUGH THIS DARKENED MAZE

BABY

TIRED OF BEING BABY-FED
SICK OF BEING PHOTOGRAHED LIKE A BABY'S HEAD

THE DIAPER IS DIRTY, TIME FOR A CHANGE
I NEED MORE THAN WET TOWELS TO CLEAN-UP, TO REARRANGE

WE ALL SHOP AND WE ALL BUY…
TO PICK AND CHOSE DOLLARED-DESIRES IS THE ART OF LIFE

MY HEAD WIRING…
IT MUST BE MISS-FIRING
TOO MANY NEWBORN-PLANS
I'M AN INFANT'S PACIFIER IN SOMEONE ELSE'S HANDS

EVERYONE SEEMS TO BE SIPPING FROM THE SOUR BREAST OF VANITY
CAN"T WE JUST TAKE A BREAK AND STEP-AWAY FROM THE INSANITY

EXTRA

ANOTHER COLLEGE DEGREE WON'T MAKE YOU HAPPY…
NEITHER WILL ALL THAT MONEY…

IT IS SO HARD TO ADMIRE THE ACTIVITIES YOU HATE
BUT I GUESS YOU ATTRIBUTE ALL SIMPLE THINGS TO FATE

YOU DIDN'T SELL YOUR SOUL AND YOU DIDN'T BUY ART
YOU JUST HELD ONTO YOUR WALLET AND MADE IT YOUR HEART

A BLUE-SUIT NEIGHBORHOOD…
SUNGLASSES THAT MAKE YOU FEEL SO GOOD

YOU SPIRAL DOWN…
YOUR THOUGHTS…OH WHAT A GLITTER-TOWN

HAND IN MY FACE, YOU BELIEVE THAT YOU CAN SIMPLY ERASE
ALL THAT WAS US…IS NOW JUST EMPTY SPACE

YOU'VE GOT SUPERSTORE LOVE…
ANY VARIETY THAT ONE CAN THINK OF

SO MANY COLORS ON YOUR DESKTOP
ALONG WITH A LIST OF PEOPLE THAT YOU'D LIKE TO STOP

YOU LIVE ON THE SECOND FLOOR, THE ANGELS AND THE FALLEN ABOVE AND
BELOW…
YOU'VE BEEN DEAD BEFORE…UNDER A HALF-MOON WITH A DEVILED GLOW

SOMETIMES YOU SEE THE WORLD IN A STRAIGHT LINE
THE CARS AND TRUCKS, LUCK AND LIFE…ALL PAUSED FOR A STOP SIGN

REMEMBER, SOME DRINKS YOU NEED TO STIR LIGHTLY…
BEWARE THE HEART AND HEAD WHICH ARE PAIRED TOO TIGHTLY

UNTITLED

WISHING, REMINISCING…MY CHIN JUST ABOVE LOVE'S FLOOD
MY HEART NO LONGER BEATS FOUR-TIME, INSTEAD IT SEARCHES FOR NEW BLOOD

OUR PASSION, PRESSURE THAT WAS NEVER REALLY STABLE
SEPARATION ACTING AS AN ASSASSIN…KILLING WHEN ABLE

WICKED ARE THE RULES OF THIS BOARD GAME…
THE OUTCOME SEEMS TO ALWAYS BE THE SAME

IDEAS CAN GREET YOU WITH OPEN ARMS OR CLOSED FISTS
CONSEQUENCES LIKE HILLS CAN IMPEDE OR ASSIST

SOMETIMES I SHIVER AND HIDE…
NO HOT SHOWER OR COFFEE CAN WARM THE INSIDE

RIGHT NOW I'M JUMPING FROM YET HANGING ONTO A LEDGE
WONDERING IF WHAT I DO AND GIVE IS SIMPLY A GUILT PLEDGE

I WON'T LET YOU IN TO FILL THIS SPACE
JUST WALK BESIDE ME UNTIL I FIND THE STRENGTH TO REPLACE…LOVE

WANT TO POUND MY STAKE INTO THE CONCRETE EARTH
MAKE SURE I'VE GOT A PLACE TO CALL HOME, A SENSE OF WORTH

LIFE IN A BOTTLE…THERE'S ONLY ONE TASTE
A 360 VIEW THAT LEADS BACK TO YOU…COMMONLY FACED

NO SLEEP LAST NIGHT…
THE DREAMS SPLIT THEIR SEEMS AND I LOST MY SIGHT

UNTITLED

THE GREEN LIGHTS MAKE YOU GO
...BUT A CRIMSON TWINGE COLORS BELOW

CHECK-MARK LOVE IS THE WAY YOU GRADE
YOUR LOVERS...TESTS, YOUR AFFECTIONS A PARADE

THE GIFTS PRESENTED WERE UNWRAPPED THEN SMASHED
THE PIECES INSIDE REPRESENT YOUR BLACKENED PAST

THE ROTATION OF YOUR CLOTHING PROJECTS BOREDOM
YOUR WISDOM...A MOUNTAIN OF HURT FOR SOME

A PROJECTION OF THINGS KNOWN AND THEN FORGOTTEN
YOUR PULSE IS LIKE A CORPSE, YOUR HEART ROTTEN

YOUR PAINT, AN OILY COLOR MIXED IN SOUR
DECEITFUL WAYS...YOUR POTENTIAL POWER

YOU PEDDLE YOUR PERSONA LIKE A TALK SHOW
SEMI-SWEET IS THE OFFER YOUR GUESTS KNOW

YOU SAID TO ME...THERE ARE NO GIVERS
I SAID I GAVE YOU EVERYTHING,...WHAT'S THE DIFFERENCE

UNTITLED

DISAPPOINTMENT, IT'S A PYRAMID…
CIRCUMSTANCE THE BASE, SUFFERING THE LID

YOUR WANTS NOW LEFT SLEEPING NEXT TO FATE
NAKED AMBITIONS ARE NEVER REALIZED WHEN LATE

YOU TRY TO SWAY LIFE'S CERTAIN SWINGS…
CAUSE YOU'LL NEVER BE OPEN TO INDIRECT THINGS

BLACK-HOLE-DIGGING ARE YOU…
SWIMMING DEEPER AND DEEPER INTO A SELFISH HUE

YOUR FACE SEPARATED BY A GRIN OF PAIN…
DON'T YOU KNOW DEEP THOUGHTS DROWN A SHALLOW BRAIN

WHY ARE THE EVENTS YOU COURT SUCH A SURPRISE
EVEN THE BLIND CAN SEE THE LEDGE AND THE MOUNTAIN'S SIZE

YOUR LANGUAGE, ONE WHERE WORDS FAIL TO SPEAK
YOUR MOVEMENTS CLOCK-LIKE AS THEY MOVE CIRCULAR…BOTTOM TO PEAK

OH, THE CRUMBLED BRIDGES YOU CAN NO LONGER CROSS…
AND YOUR BREAD…NOW CRUST, HANGS HIGH WITHOUT SAUCE

IS IT THE TAIL WHICH MAKES A DEVIL SUCH A SHAMED BEAST
OR THE APPETITE OF ONE'S EYES AS THEY GLANCE AT THE FEAST

UNTITLED

MONEY, IT'S A CONFIDENCE…
YOU DECORATE ME WITH YOUR CHAIN-LINK FENCE

YOU SAY, THE KEY IS LOOKING LIKE YOU KNOW YOUR PLACE
…TAKE HOLD AND SCULPT YOUR OWN FREE–SPACE

I SAY, INTER-WEAVE YOUR DECISIONS WITH SOME TENDER ACTION
…THEN PUT THOSE FEELINGS INTO A BLENDER WITH SATISFACTION

YOU RESPOND TO CARROTS HUNG AT EYE LEVEL
CHOOSE YOUR SUIT, ANGEL-WINGS OR TAILED-DEVIL

WHERE IS THE PLACE THAT YOU WISH TO LIVE
HEART AND HEAD BOTH EMPTY…BEEN BLED LIKE A SIEVE

STRUCTURE…A VISITOR YOU PASS ON THE STREET
ATTITUDE IS YOUR APPETITE, GRITTY FEELINGS KEPT NEAT

YOUR IDEAS REST ON SQUARE SHOULDERS AND TIGHTLY BENT LIPS
THIS STRAIN IRRITATES YOUR EYES AND LENGTHENS YOUR FINGERTIPS

YOUR HANDS BRING NOTHING TO OUR SHRINE
YET YOU STEAL THE BREAD AND DRINK THE WINE

TO BE EXPOSED AS WEAK OR SUCH…WOULD BE ENTIRELY TOO MUCH
IF LESS THAN COLD WOULD THEY TAKE AWAY YOUR SOCIAL CRUTCH

UNTITLED

TO BREAK-AWAY FROM YOU IS LIKE RIPPING SKIN
THE SPILLING OF WINE FROM OUR CUP IS A LOVE-SIN

ANY ALTITUDE WAS MY ATTITUDE UNTIL I CRASHED INTO PAIN
THE HURT THAT I NOW KNOW REMINDS ME NOT TO JUMP FROM A GOOD PLANE

IT WAS WRONG TO RUN MILES THAT PAVED THE ROADS AHEAD
MY THOUGHTS UNCERTAIN, MY HEAD BEHIND A CURTAIN, FEELINGS UN-WED

I WANTED TO PULL OUR DREAMS FROM THE CLOUDS IN THE SKY…
NOW I'LL NEVER HOLD THEM, NEVER GET A CHANCE TO SOLIDIFY (OUR LOVE)

THANK GOD I WILL ALWAYS HAVE YOU LIVING IN MY HEART
IF EVEN JUST TO PRETEND, MY BRUSH WILL STILL PAINT YOUR ART

PLEASE KEEP TAKING NOTES FOR YOURSELF, YOUR GIFTS DESERVE THE BEST
ENJOY THE PARODY OF WHAT WAS ONCE A LOVE-AND-US TEST

I'LL FOREVER PICK-UP THE PHONE AND HOPE THAT IT IS YOU
I'LL PRAY YOU ARE NEVER ALONE AND ASK GOD TO BRIGHTEN THE VIEW

MAYBE, SOMEDAY, WE'LL BOTH BE HOME WITH THE BRICKS AND STONE
MAYBE, SOMEDAY, OUR SOULS WILL BE FREE FROM THE LIPS AND FINGERTIPS
OF FEARS UNKNOWN

ONE, TWO, THREE

THE WINTER MONTHS CAN BE SO UNFEELING
A SOUL'S FIRE BURNS LOW WITHOUT FUEL FOR HEALING

I NEED THE WARMTH WE HAD
I MISS BEING THE SPARK YOU CLAD

A PERSON STAYS IN MOTION UNTIL CONTACT IS MET
WE USED TO TURN TOGETHER AS WHEELS IN A SET

DID I DIG THE HOLES TOO DEEP
DID I FALL ASLEEP
MISSING THE REACH OF YOUR HAND
CHAINS NOW TANGLE THE LINK THAT ONCE BAND

SPACE, IT CREATES A NEED TO BE FILLED
A HEART, WEALTH THAT TENDS TO BE WILLED

CLOSE IS THE SAME AS NOT AT ALL
GRABBING SOMETHING YOU CAN'T SHARE ISN'T WORTH GRASPING AT ALL

TO PRESERVE THE MOMENT…THAT IS THE GOAL
TO SHARE THE SHADOWED SECRETS KEPT CORNERED IN YOUR SOUL

WAITING TO SING THE SONGS WE COMPOSED
WANTING TO OPEN THE DOORS WE CLOSED
TO CENTER MYSELF AS YOUR SUN
TO FIND THAT NEED TO BECOME ONE

MIND CLUTTER…
SPIRITUAL MUTTER…

HOW TO GET WHAT YOU PERCEIVE
HOW TO HANG ON TO WHAT YOU BELIEVE

SHOULD THE REACH EXCEED THE GRASP
SHOULD THE FUTURE EXCLUDE THE PAST

THE HEART IS A KEEPER OF TERMS, NOT TIME
AN ASSERTION OF WAR OR TREATY TO BE SIGNED
FAILURE TO COMPLY IS NEVER A CHOICE
LIFE SHOULD BE DIRECTED BY THIS LOVE VOICE

POEMS

(OTHER)

THE GAME

THE STARTER RAISES HIS GUN, YOU TAKE YOUR PLACE
WE ALL LINE UP SOMETIME, TAKING OUR SHOT WINNING THE RACE

WHAT IS YOUR TRAINING SPEED…TORTOISE OR HARE
WHAT ARE YOUR GOALS IN LIFE, DO YOU REALLY CARE

HAVE YOU EVER BROKEN A SWEAT
HAVE YOU EVER PLACED A BET…WHAT DO YOU WANT TO GET

LIFE IT'S YOUR GAME
IT CAN WIELD GREATNESS OR IT CAN SUIT SHAME
IS IT PASSING YOU ON THE RIGHT
OR ARE YOU DRIVING WITH ARCADIA IN SIGHT

MUSCLE AND FINESSE ARE ITEMS YOU WILL NEED
BUT A TRIMMED APPETITE AND SPACIOUS SIGHT WILL HELP YOU SUCCEED

SEVER TIES WITH THOSE WHO HOLD YOU BACK
RIDE THE BUS MARKED "ATTAINMENT " INTO THE BLACK

OVERTAKE YOUR DREAMS LIKE YOU ACQUIRE MONEY
INVEST, DIVERSIFY…TASTE THE PREFERRED HONEY

LIFE IT'S YOUR GAME
BETTER RAISE YOUR GUN AND TAKE AIM
POUR YOUR FOUNDATION TO SUPPORT BELIEF
DESTROY YOUR BRIDGES TO DROWN THE GRIEF

DON'T LET DOUBT BUILD-UP IN YOUR HEART
ALWAYS BELIEVE, THAT IF YOU PERCEIVE…IT WON'T FALL APART

DON'T BE AFRAID TO STEP-OFF THE ROOF CALLED SHAME
BEGIN THE GAME, WIN THE GAME, WIN YOUR GAME…

IN-BETWEEN

FEELING AS IF YOU'RE UNBORN
TOSSED ABOUT BY BEFORE AND AFTER
BROKEN BARRICADES NO LONGER WARN
AND GOD HAS TURNED-AWAY IN LAUGHTER

NOW YOU'RE TRYING TO BE HOLY
PRAYING, GIVING, LIVING MORE SLOWLY
TURNING OVER AS IF SOIL IN A FIELD
HOPING A BETTER IMAGE IS WHAT YOU'LL YIELD

MATERIALS…
SHALLOW IDEALS
WHAT YOU THINK YOU NEED
ALL IS TURNING TO GREED

IF YOU PLOW EVIL, IT WILL BE ALL THAT YOU SEW
IF YOU COLLECT FROM THE DEVIL, DEUS WILL SURELY KNOW
NOTHING FROM YOUR LABOR WILL YOU TAKE IN YOUR HAND
ALL TURNS TO DUST WHEN YOU'RE LAID IN THE LAND

COLD WINDS COME AND GO, YOUR COURSE WAVES
SINNERS PURCHASE WHAT THEY KNOW, BUT IT NEVER SAVES
HEY…WHAT'S YOUR OBJECT OF SECURITY
HOW LONG WILL YOU LIVE IN OBSCURITY

ARE YOU RIDING THE MONEY TRAIN
ARE YOU LIVING FOR GAIN
KEEP COUNTING YOUR GOLD
I'LL STEAL IT WHEN YOUR OLD

DISHONESTY, YOUR FORMER PHILOSOPHY
INSINCERITY NOW BECOMES YOUR ATROCITY
REMEMBER, ROSES ALWAYS DIE WHEN PLANTED IN SAND
AND FUTURES WILL VARY WHEN RARELY PLANNED

ROMANS TWELVE, NINE....CORINTHIANS THIRTEEN
IS EVERYTHING FINE...EVERYTHING SERENE
WHO FORGIVES AND WHO FORGETS...
WILL YOU LEAVE THIS WORLD WITHOUT REGRETS

INKPEN

WHITE PAPER, BLACK PEN
I'M WRITING TO GOD AGAIN

THOUGHTS RISE LIKE SMOKE
TO MANY...SOMETIMES I CHOKE

TYPE "A" PERSONALITY...OFTEN CLOUDS WHAT I SEE
DON'T KNOW WHO I AM, JUST WHO I WANT TO BE

YOU GIVE...YOU GET
WILL I CLEAR THE SUCCESS BAR YOU SET
OPEN ARMS WHEN TOO WIDE...CAN'T RECEIVE
CLOSED CONCEPTS TREAD SHALLOW WHEN IN REPRIEVE

RAINY DAYS AND COLD CHILLS
WOMEN HANG-OVERS COLLIDE WITH COFFEE SPILLS

I INHALE THE AIR...AND YOU TOO
I OFTEN WONDER JUST WHAT IS TRUE

SOMETIMES BUILT INTO A CORNER BY YOUR CONSTRUCTION
MY STABILITY, A HOUSE OF CARDS...I FEEL THE SUCTION

SHAME, DON'T COUNT IT OUT
IT CLEARS YOUR VISION NO DOUBT
LET IT SET YOUR BOUNDARIES...IT WILL BOX YOU IN
KILL IT AND YOU WILL SURELY SIN

SOME DAYS I GET EVERYTHING I WANT
SOME DAYS I RECOIL, GET CORNERED AND DAUNT

CAN I EVER HEAL THIS FLESH MACHINE
MAKE IT RULE IN UNION LIKE A KING AND QUEEN

INK, BLACK...BLUE...RED
MY PEN RIGHTS WHAT WAS ONCE SAID
OH...THE THOUGHTS THAT NEED TO BE READ
IS IT ALL INTENDED TO BE DEAD

LIFE

I CAN FEEL THE ADRENALINE...UNDER MY SKIN
HERE COMES THE WORLD TO TAKE A SWING AGAIN

I BETTER DUCK BEFORE I GET HIT
COULD SOMEONE SHOW ME TO THE NEAREST EXIT

LIFE USED TO MEAN WITH BREATH COMES CHANCE
NOW IT MEANS TOO LITTLE CANS AND TOO MANY CAN'TS

CAN WE BREAK-FREE OF THE THINGS THAT BIND
REGAIN WHAT WE ONCE LEFT BEHIND
CHALLENGE THOSE WHO GET IN OUR WAY
ILLUMINATE THE DARKEST OF GRAY

WHO SAID YOU'LL NEVER SUCCEED...
CONQUER THE NEGATIVITY ON WHICH THEY FEED

WE GET SOFT WHEN COMFORT COMES
BECOME PREOCCUPIED WITH ASSETS AND SUMS

SKETCH YOUR FUTURE TO YOUR DESIGN
REASON, REFRAIN FROM EXCESSIVE GAIN, GET ALIGNED

MAINTAINING YOUR ENERGY THAT IS THE KEY
DESIRE SHOULD BE THE FIRE BURNING RAPIDLY
THE ART OF HAVING FAITH YOU MUST MASTER
CREATE YOUR OWN SUCCESS, DISPEL DISASTER

EVENTS WILL HAPPEN IN SUCCESSION
PATIENCE IS PRESENCE, A VALUABLE LESSON

I NEED NEW STIMULI TO FEEL
BUT TIME OFTEN CUTS AS IT HEALS

GOD GIVE ME STRENGTH TO RISE ABOVE INIQUITY
HELP ME FIND THE COURAGE TO CHANGE AND THE EYES TO FORESEE

TARGET

LOVE FIND ME A TARGET
LET ME PLACE MY BET

THE WALLS INSIDE MUST FALL BEFORE THOSE ABROAD
CEMENT STRUCTURES ARE LIKE PAPER AGAINST AN EMOTIONAL FACADE

THEY SAY THE STRONG FEED ON THE WEEK
BUT THE HUNTERS CAN'T ALWAYS SEE THE PREY THEY SEEK

GOLD LOVES THE COMPANY OF GOLD
I CAN'T REMEMBER ALL OF THE MEMORIES I'VE SOLD
SANITY SOMETIMES FADES FROM BLACK TO RED
AS INNOCENT AND GUILTY THOUGHTS LECTURE IN MY HEAD

FIRES ALWAYS RETURN TO THEIR SPARK
CAN ANYONE CONTROL THE FLAME WHICH LIGHTENS THE DARK

A SIMPLE ACT WILL SOMETIMES GIVE BIRTH TO WONDER
TOO MANY TIMES THE IMPRESSIVE INSTINCT PULLS US UNDER

IS MY AIM TOO LOW OR MY SIGHTS TOO HIGH
SHOULD I BE POINTING MY ARROWS INTO THE SKY

WILL I EVER KNOW LOVE'S PROTOCOL
HOW MANY TIMES MUST I TAKE THE FALL
OH, LET ME BECOME A USUAL SUSPECT…
PASSION-CHARGED IMPRISONED IN HER NET

GLASS CAN OFTEN BE YOUR HEART'S CASING
IT WILL SOMETIMES MAGNIFY THE TROUBLES YOU'RE FACING

OH…TO SEASON LIFE WITH SUGAR NOT SALT
IS FAILURE IN LOVE REALLY ANYONE'S FAULT

THE FUTURE WILL ONLY BECOME WHAT YOU DESIRE IT TO BE
DESTINATIONS ONLY SURFACE WHEN PATHS CHANGE THEIR ITINERARY

ORLANDO

GRABBED A PLANE FROM CHICAGO
GOIN' DOWN TO ORLANDO…

THE TAXIS COST YOU THIRTY ONE-WAY
AND THE SUN ONLY SHINES IF YOU PAY

HERE YOU CAN DREAM IN ENGLISH OR SPANISH
WHITE HOUSE GREEN WILL PAVE ANY WISH

THE HUMIDITY CLINGS LIKE SYRUP TO A BISCUIT
THE QUESTION ISN'T HOW…BUT WHEN TO DIP IT
LUSH GREEN IS THE BACKDROP TO EVERY SCENE
MAGICAL KINGDOMS CALLED TIME-SHARES, IMITATION BYZANTINE

CONCRETE CONVENTIONS SIXTY-THOUSAND STRONG
MEMORIES BUILT ON VACATION-SLABS ONE WEEK LONG

LET ME CELEBRATE THIS ADVENTURE, HAND ME A CIGAR
WAIT…IT'S ONLY NINE-THIRTY, YOU CAN'T SMOKE IN THIS PLEASURE ISLAND BAR

HEY WHERE'S THE HOUSE OF THAT TIGER WOODS GUY
TAKE ME TO THE STRIP-CLUB, ON SECOND THOUGHT…JUST DRIVE BYE

PALM TREES AND A WARM BREEZE
CAN I HAVE ANOTHER YARD OF BEER…PLEASE
SOUTHERN CITY BUT LITTLE SOUTHERN CHARM
CASH-STATION BLUES, UNINTENTIONAL HARM

OR…LANDO, OR…NOT
MAN, MY TEMPERATURE IS HOT

THIS EXPERIENCE I'M SURE IS NOT THE NORM
I HOPE TO RETURN NEXT TIME WITHOUT THE STORM

LOOKING

LOOKING FOR A LOVE THAT WILL TAKE YOU HIGHER
CAN WE REALLY RISE LIKE SMOKE FROM A FIRE

DO YOU FEAR LOVE
DO YOU FEAR THE GREAT GOD ABOVE

WE ALL WEAR ARMOR…
EVEN IF YOU'RE A DECEIVER, BELIEVER OR CHARMER

YOU HOLD ONTO EMOTIONS TO SEE HOW THEY FEEL
HOW DO YOU KNOW IF THEY ARE EVER REAL
SHOULD A GOOD MOMENT LAST LONGER THAN A BAD
AS A SERVANT ONE ALWAYS WANTS WHAT ANOTHER HAS HAD

WILL LOVE EVER CAMP ON YOUR PORCH STAIRS
WILL IT COMPLICATE YOUR AFFAIRS OR COMPLEMENT YOUR CARES

DOES THE EXPERIENCE NEED TO EXPLODE LIKE THE FOURTH OF JULY
IF IT DOESN'T…WILL YOU STILL GIVE PASSION'S BOARDGAME A TRY

SWEETNESS DOESN'T GUARANTEE PERFECT TASTE
AND YOUR TRASH CAN'T ALWAYS BE CONSIDERED WASTE

PICK-UP LOVE, IT'S BAGGED AT THE END OF YOUR DRIVEWAY
REMEMBER ALL THOSE HOPEFUL PHRASES YOU USED TO SAY
DON'T FORGET TO USE THE INSTRUMENTS YOU ONCE LEARNED TO PLAY
OH…WHEN IS THE LAST TIME YOU KNELT TO PRAY…FOR LOVE

SPECIAL TIMES, SPECIAL DISEASE
YOU GET NO RESPONSE WHEN YOU DON'T SAY PLEASE

YOU SEEM TO SAVOR THE THINGS YOU'VE COLLECTED
HEART-BREAK WAS NEVER THE GUEST YOU EXPECTED

YOU WANT TO MOVE BUT CAN'T FIND A NEW PEARCH
WILL FATE ALLOW YOU ENOUGH LIGHT TO CONTINUE THE SEARCH

HOW LONG WILL YOU WAIT TO BE BAPTIZED NEW
AREN'T THESE FEELINGS JUST SPRINGTIME RESIDUE
CAN'T YOU CATCH A STAR IF YOU WEAR A GLOVE
WILL YOU FOREVER BE AN OBSERVER, WILL YOU EVER BE IN LOVE

STRIPPED

HARDENED SHELL, SOFTER CORE
OH…DON'T YOU DESERVE SO MUCH MORE

DO YOUR BARRICADES BARRICADE YOU
DO YOU THINK THEY NEED TOO

WHO OWNS YOUR PASSION…YOU OR THE DREAM
EVER EXCEEDED THE LIMITS, EVER FORCED THE SEAM

ENTERTAIN THOUGHTS ANEW
UNEARTH YOUR DIAMONDS, SHOVEL AWAY THICKENED RESIDUE
PLEASE OPEN YOUR DOORWAY
LET WHAT CAME BEFORE SLIP AWAY

I WANT TO WALK THESE TRACKS WITH YOU
TRAVEL TO YOUR HEART AND UNPACK SOMEWHERE NEW

DON'T SELL YOUR EMOTIONS LIKE MERCHANDISE
LET YOUR TOUGHENED WALLS DISSOLVE LIKE ICE

I'LL DO ANYTHING TO QUICKEN YOUR DROWNING CADENCE
LET YOURSELF FEED IN GREEN PASTURES, JUMP OVER THE FENCE

STRIP FROM YOUR SKIN…YOUR SIN
LET YELLOW DIVERSIONS STRENGTHEN
OPEN THE SHELVES THAT HOUSE YOUR PAIN
DON'T DEPRIVE EMOTIONS THAT GRANT YOU GAIN

YOUR DESIRES BRIGHTEN LIKE GOLD…WHEN EXPOSED
WHY WOULD YOU EVER INSIST ON BEING SO CLOSED

DISBAND YOUR BATTLE LINES…AS THEY ONLY CAUSE WAR
UNVEIL THAT WHICH WAS PULLED BY THE SEA AND SUNKEN FAR FROM SHORE

RISEN

SATELLITE PERCHED…
THE CROW BEGINS HIS HURRIED SEARCH

TO FIND AND TO FILL THAT HOLE
A TRAIN-TUNNEL OF HUNGER IN HIS SOUL

SEE THE MOTH STEP-RISE TO THE LIGHT
A STREET-LAMP WOMB ACTS AS THE MOON CUTTING THE NIGHT

RISE-UP, TAKE FLIGHT
WE'RE ALL WINGED CREATURES TONIGHT
AS NEED DICTATES YOUR COURSE
REMEMBER…DESIRE IS A PURCHASED GUIDE-FORCE

A PLANE LIFTS ITS NOSE TO THE SUN
STEERED BY A COMPASS THAT CLAIMS TO KNOW DIRECTION

DO WE EVER REALLY KNOW THE DARK SHADOWS WHICH FLESH-ORBIT
WILL THE BLEACHED-LIGHT DISTILL THE DARKNESS AND ABSORB IT

STEAM WILL FOREVER ESCAPE FROM YOUR MOUTH–PRISON
IT NEEDS TO ONCE AGAIN RE-MARRY THE AIR, REVERSE THE FISSION

SLOWLY LOOK-UP
SIP FROM YOUR CODDLED CUP
DOES ONE AMASS WEALTH THROUGH COLLECTION
OR DO THE GEMSTONES OF LIFE ARRIVE BY WAY OF REFLECTION

EMOTIONS SURFACE LIKE A SWIMMER FOR AIR
WHITE-CAPPED WAVES CRASH AGAINST THE ROCK OF DESPAIR

DO YOU CONTINUE TO HANG ABOVE IT ALL
IS IT YOUR NECK OR FINGER-TIPS WHICH PREVENTS YOUR FALL

WE ALL ASCEND WHEN OUR BURDENS LIGHTEN
ALWAYS TO CONTEND WITH WHAT APPEARS TO FRIGHTEN

ARE YOU RISEN....
IF NOT SO.... WHEN
WILL THE CHANGE SOON BEGIN
...ENTER IN

HEADACHE

STUCK IN TRAFFIC, THEREFORE I AM
STEEL BODIES MOVE LIKE SWINE TO THEIR SLAUGHTER…TASTE THE HAM

MY FOOT TAPS TO MY BRAIN-WAVES
THAT BUMPER STICKER SHOUTS…ONLY JESUS SAVES

I FEEL THE STRUGGLE AND WEIGHT OF MY SOUL
WILL IT RETREAT WHEN I REACH MY GOAL

TOO MUCH SUNLIGHT THEY SAY WILL BLIND
TOO MANY THOUGHTS PAY RENT TO MY MIND
I OFTEN WANT TO LEAVE, BUT KNOWN DESTINATIONS DECEIVE
WHAT CAN I ACHIEVE, WHAT CAN I BELIEVE…

PAIN WILL MAKE YOUR FOCUS INTENSE
IT WILL MAKE YOU REALIZE YOUR WEAKEST DEFENSE

HELLO…MY HALO IS HOLLOW
WHEN MY HEART LEADS SHOULD MY HEAD ALWAYS FOLLOW

WILD-FIRE IN MY BLOOD
EMOTIONS OVERCOME AND OFTEN FLOOD

OH THE GRASS ISN'T GREENER
VIEWS JUST LOOK DIFFERENT CLEANER
HOLES ARE CIRCLES ON THE OUTER EDGE
BALCONIES…SPRINGBOARDS OF WHICH DREAMS CLING TO THE LEDGE

I CAN DO ANYTHING WITH A GOOD SONG BEHIND ME
LIFT A MOUNTAIN, PUNCH THE SKY, SWIM THE SEA..WHERE IS THE OPPORTUNITY

IS IT EVER THE RIGHT-TIME TO MOVE
IS IT EVER REALLY NECESSARY TO IMPROVE

I'LL SEE WHAT HAPPENS AS I STIR THE MIX
ADDING CHANGE TO THE BATTER…THROWING IT AGAINST THE WALL TO SEE WHAT
STICKS

LOVE

IF YOU CROSS THE STREET OF LOVE, BETTER LOOK BOTH WAYS
EMOTIONS WON'T ALWAYS FIND AN ESCAPE FROM THIS MAZE

LOVE…LEAD AND FOLLOW, HEART AND MIND ARE NEVER FULL
LOVE…CAN LEAVE YOU EMPTY, HOLLOW AND UNBEAUTIFUL

JUST AS WATER CAN BE COLD AND ROUGH
LOVE CAN PULL YOU UNDER, IT CAN CALL YOUR BLUFF
LOVE IT'S NOT SUPPOSED TO MAKE YOU SANE
IT NEVER PROMISED FREEDOM FROM PAIN

LOVE COMES AND GOES ITS TARGET THE JUGULAR
WHERE IS THAT HUNGER YOU USED TO KNOW, WILL IT EVER REOCCUR

LONGING FOR OLD PASSION AND LOST DESIRE
WAITING TO BUILD AN UPWARD ATTITUDE THEN SET IT ON FIRE

NO FEELING LEFT IN THIS HEART-SPACE
LOVE'S TRAPPED YOU IN THIS DARK UNFORGIVING PLACE
HANDS THAT ONCE BUILT NOW DESTROY
MEMORIES CAN'T RETRIEVE FORGOTTEN JOY

LOVE…LESSONS YOU LEARN, PAY THE PRICE
LOVE…INVERTED TURNS AND SACRIFICE

IF THE HONEY HAS SOURED, PASS THE VINEGAR
YOU'LL NEVER DRINK ALONE EVERYONE HAS BEEN HERE

LOVE…IT CAN TURN AROUND
SOMEDAY YOU'LL RECOVER WHAT WAS ONCE FOUND
TAKE HER HAND, IGNORE WHAT YOU'VE HEARD
BUT REMEMBER, LOVE IS NEVER PLANNED…NEVER INSURED

DOUBT

DOUBT, IT SOMETIMES FADES IN AND OUT
NO CASH...TOO MANY BETS MADE WITHOUT

SHE SAYS GOOD NIGHT, BUT UNDER-BREATH SHE SAYS GOOD-BYE
SOME PEOPLE RUN WHEN THE CLOUDS FADE FROM THEIR SKY

A STEAMING DAY, ONE THAT WON'T WASH AWAY
TOO HOT TO THE SKIN TO WIN,...TO PLAY

AT TIMES TROUBLE,...BLUE TWISTS TO BLACK
THE TAPPING FINGERS OF FAILURE ON MY BACK

I MAY HAVE LOST MY WAY, STEPPED BEYOND THE LINE
FORGOTTEN ABOUT THE DAY, SWALLOWED TOO MUCH WINE

SHADOWS AGAINST WHITE WALLS ONLY BRINGS GRAY
ENTRANCES TO EXIT SIGNS, THESE FEELINGS NEVER STAY

SHORT-TIME AND SHORTCOMINGS, FLAVORS I NOW TASTE
THEY SAY SWALLOW SOME MORE PRIDE, SWIM IN MORE WASTE

YOU CAN SHELVE FRAGILE FEELINGS ONLY IF STORAGE WILL PERMIT
DELICATE HANDS OPEN TO GREET AND HEAVY HANDS CLOSE TO HIT

SUBSTANDARD LIVING...
EFFORTS PUT FORTH ONLY HALF-GIVING

EVIDENCE OF SLEEPING THOUGHT
SIGNS OF DREAMS STILL NOT YET CAUGHT

EYES SO RED...THE COLOR NOW BECOMES THE VIEW
LOCKED IN A BOX WHERE ONLY THE FUTURE GLOWS NEW

SUCCESS, AH...AN INDIVIDUAL HIGH-BAR
MEASURE YOUR STICK WITH THE MAN WHO HAS THE SHINY, BLUE CAR

UNTITLED

CHOCOLATE SPILLED ONTO PORCELAIN
DARK HANDS ON LIGHT SKIN

A FACE SELDOM SEEN BY THESE EYES
LIKE A MOUNTAIN NEXT TO NOTHINGNESS…A VISUAL SURPRISE

HER LOVE BRINGS ARMIES ONTO THE HILLS
LIKE DESERT-SUNSHINE IT BEATS DOWNWARD…BREAKING ALL WILLS

I LOVE THE DARKNESS WHEN MY EYES BEGIN TO CLOSE
THE FEEL OF COTTON WHEN SCENTED BY A SEASONED ROSE

THESE SHEETS THAT WE SHARE HAVE THE POWER TO DISMISS
WALLS TO THE WORLD THEY CAN HONOR OR REJECT ANY WISH

I STARE INTO YOU AND AM RIPPLED BY WHAT'S REFLECTED
I HOPE MY INTENTIONS AREN'T EVER MISDIRECTED

SOLITUDE ONLY SUITS THE SOUR OF HEART
COLORS CHOOSE YOU TO LAYER CANVAS IN ART

DON'T YOU SEE I WANT TO BECOME YOUR MIXING PALETTE
WILL YOU DESIGN MY APARTMENT IN THE COLOR OF A SUNSET

UNTITLED

IF WATER IS LOVE, I'M ONLY KNEE DEEP
TO KEEP MY HEAD ABOVE…YOU STAND ME ON CONCRETE

YOU DON'T WANT ME TOO WET OR TOO DRY
YOU JUST WANT EVERYTHING ABOUT WAIST HIGH

NEUTRAL…A POSITION WHICH FEELS SAFE TO YOU
…THERE'S NO SYSTEM TO THE THINGS YOU DO

TWIN SISTER, WHAT HAPPENED TO THE OTHER HALF
WHY MUST YOU LEAN ON LOVE, TURN…THEN LAUGH

SHAKE ME AND SPRAY ME LIKE A CANNED BEVERAGE
WAKE ME THEN LAY ME WITH PLANNED LEVERAGE

BOTOM LINES…QUESTIONS YOU NEVER DEFINE
STEREO VOICES IN YOUR HEAD CONTINUE TO DINE

YOU SKIP OVER THE CRACKS IN OUR HIGHWAY
AND YOU PAVE OUR CHANCE WITH HOPE IN DECAY

WHAT RISES WITHIN YOU BESIDES BLACK SMOKE
WHAT CAN YOU EXPECT TO GAIN WHEN YOU REACH TO CHOKE

SUBSTANCES SEEM TO BE YOUR WEAK LINK
OPEN DOORS CAN CAUSE YOUR HEAD TO THINK

UNTITLED

YOU CAN PAINT BY NUMBERS IF YOU PAINT ME RED
STATUES AND CELLOPHANE DECORATE THE PLAYGROUND IN MY HEAD

SEARCHING FOR THAT DROPPED CLUE YOU LEFT BEHIND
THAT LETTER THAT YOU LEFT HIDDEN, STILL UNSIGNED

…GAMES THAT HAD NO BOARDS, PIECES OR RULES
BLAME…A MIXTURE OF HURT, THE UNKNOWN AND FOOLS

THE SUNSHINE THAT BLINDED NOW WARMS MY BACK
I CAN'T DECIDE IF YOU WERE MY FRIEND OR A WOLF-PACK

LEFT TO DANGLE ON THE OUTER EDGE
A CURIOUS ANGLE WHEN YOU HANG FROM A BROKEN PLEDGE

YOU LIVE IN FEAR AND YOU DON'T HOLD ANY HANDS
LISTENING TO WHAT YOU HEAR, YOUR BODY RARELY STANDS

DIPPING YOUR HEART INTO BLACK PAINT
ISN'T THE TIME SPENT MIXED BY THINGS THAT TAINT

I OPEN MY EYES TO CHECK YOUR POSITION
I OFTEN WONDER WHAT YOU'RE WISHIN'

A THOUGHT

If a flower lives and blooms in the company of other flowers, why when picked, especially by the wrong picker, does the splendor of the flower begin to wilt, fade and eventually die. In my opinion, a flower surrounded by other flowers, accustomed to the nourishment of the soil, in the company of others of similar like and similar attributes, only gives and enhances the flower's sense of belonging. No matter how well the picker cares for or does not care for the flower, the end result is still death. No fancy vase, no chemical nutrients and certainly no faux climate settings will ever replace or re-train the flowers' sense of origin, comfort and/or the growth it once knew. Just because a flower, to a picker, seemingly begs to be picked as it brilliantly reveals itself to the world, it does not mean that the flower wishes to leave the company of other flowers. Two flowers together, particularly two flowers that bloom from the same stem understand that the sharing of that same stem not only provides conjointal togetherness, but also provides life. A picker can admire, pluck and even love a flower, but a picker can never become a flower.

Just a thought…

FITZPATRICK

§

ABOUT THE AUTHOR

John Fitzpatrick was born in the Midwestern United States, just along the Mississippi River, in the blue-collar town of Moline, Illinois. John is a former collegiate swimmer, turned writer, who now lives and works just outside of Chicago. John enjoys many activities such as lifting weights, running, listening to music, reading and the study of pop-culture. John has worked previously with some well-established musicians, collaborating with his use of lyrics and rhythmic insight, to complete many songs. John would like to continue working with music industry innovators and would like to continue to branch-out further as a writer. John's creative skills include being able to change his thoughts to either reflect upon true-life instances and/or to reflect upon manufactured ones. Much like an actor transforming himself into a created role, John is a keen observer and presenter of the emotion found within himself and others. He has a rare sense of description, which includes in-depth phrases and quips, in his compositions. John is truly a young man who is worth reading in text and/or exploring in other mediums.

INDEX